The "I LOVE MY RICE COOKER"

Recipe Book

From *Mashed Sweet Potatoes* to *Spicy Ground Beef*,
175 Easy—and Unexpected—Recipes

Adams Media

New York   London   Toronto   Sydney   New Delhi

Adams Media
An Imprint of Simon & Schuster, Inc.
57 Littlefield Street
Avon, Massachusetts 02322

First Adams Media trade paperback edition JANUARY 2018

ADAMS MEDIA and colophon are trademarks of Simon and Schuster.

For information about special discounts for bulk purchases, please contact Simon & Schuster Special Sales at 1-866-506-1949 or business@simonandschuster.com.

The Simon & Schuster Speakers Bureau can bring authors to your live event. For more information or to book an event contact the Simon & Schuster Speakers Bureau at 1-866-248-3049 or visit our website at www.simonspeakers.com.

Interior design by Colleen Cunningham
Photographs by James Stefiuk

Manufactured in the United States of America

10 9 8 7 6 5 4 3 2 1

Library of Congress Cataloging-in-Publication Data
Adams Media, (firm).
The "I love my rice cooker" recipe book.
Avon, Massachusetts: Adams Media, 2018.
Series: "I Love My".
Includes index.
LCCN 2017046892 (print) | LCCN 2017050459 (ebook) | ISBN 9781507206362 (pb) | ISBN 9781507206379 (ebook)
Subjects: LCSH: Cooking (Rice) | One-dish meals. | Electric rice cookers. | LCGFT: Cookbooks.
LCC TX809.R5 (ebook) | LCC TX809.R5 I2 2018 (print) | DDC 641.6/318--dc23
LC record available at https://lccn.loc.gov/2017046892

ISBN 978-1-5072-0636-2
ISBN 978-1-5072-0637-9 (ebook)

Contains material adapted from the following title published by Adams Media, an Imprint of Simon & Schuster, Inc.: The Everything® Rice Cooker Cookbook by Hui Leng Tay, copyright © 2010, ISBN 978-1-4405-0233-0.

Contents

Introduction

Drunken Apple and Onion Pork Tenderloin.
Mushroom-Swiss Chicken Hoagies.
Blueberry Bread Pudding.
Your rice cooker isn't just for rice anymore!

Now, in the *The "I Love My Rice Cooker" Recipe Book*, in addition
to a variety of rice- and Asian-based dishes, you can prepare
culinary delicacies like Root Beer Beef Short Ribs and Orange-
Maple Chicken Legs alongside simplified versions of classics like
Steamed Asparagus with Mustard-Dill Sauce, Salmon Patties,
and even Cheeseburger Casserole! And each of the delicious
175 dishes in this book is presented with easy-to-follow instructions to help you serve these exciting and healthy meals, often
in less time than similar dishes cooked in pots and pans on the
stovetop—and with a lot less cleanup. How is the rice cooker so
versatile? Well, this simple appliance can serve as a soup pot,
a skillet, a sauté pan, a wok, and more, all in one simple-to-use,
easy-to-clean device. So if you're looking to create amazing
one-pot meals, the rice cooker is tailor-made for your kitchen.
Whether you're looking to update your list of rice cooker staples
or have just picked this appliance off the shelf, you'll soon be
able to prepare any recipe in this book with just a few minutes of
prep time. And if you just need a refresher or a beginner's course
on how to use your rice cooker, don't worry! Everything you
need to know is right in Chapter 1 of this book.

So let's get started! Before you know it you'll be all set to flip
the switch and start making these quick and easy rice cooker
recipes.

Cooking with a Rice Cooker

The rice cooker, invented in Japan in the 1950s, was one of the first electric food-preparation devices to make its way into home kitchens, which made it an instant hit. Celebrating their sudden liberation from the famously boring act of standing over a pot of rice, many home cooks began to wonder: a metal pot, sitting atop an electric heating element that progressively heats, simmers, boils, and finally cooks whatever is placed inside—what else might this gadget be able to prepare?

The answer, it turns out, is almost any dish that can be prepared in a pan over the stovetop. As millions of home cooks now know, it's entirely possible to cook an entire beef stew in a rice cooker, or a seafood soup, or just about anything else. It's all about choosing the right recipes—congratulations!—and getting comfortable with some new and easy-to-learn techniques.

By now you've heard all the raves about rice cookers and how easy it can be to prepare tasty, healthy, and satisfying dishes using just this one appliance. But if you haven't done much one-pot cooking, just how that's possible can be confusing, maybe even a little intimidating. If that's you, good news—we're happy to tell you that the opposite is true, and that cooking with your rice cooker is one of the simplest and most accessible ways to prepare a meal.

Anything worth doing takes a little bit of preparation and practice, even something as straightforward as using a rice cooker. So if you've been using your cooker just for rice, or even if you've just unboxed your first rice cooker, we've prepared this chapter to help you get started with this exciting and efficient way of cooking.

If you've already begun to explore your rice cooker's abilities, know your way around your machine, and are looking for new recipes to unlock its full potential, feel free to move right along to the recipes beginning in the next chapter—or to read on for tips and information that just might help you better understand what your rice cooker can do!

What Can Your Rice Cooker Do?

As millions of home cooks are learning, the simple, traditional rice cooker can cook almost anything a home cook would or could prepare in a pan over the stovetop. As with any other kitchen appliance, your dishes will improve as you get to know your own rice cooker. While all traditional rice cookers are based on the same basic engineering, different brands and models have their own unique features and quirks. Some cook hotter than others on the same settings, so Low or High in one pot may not be the same as in another. Most rice cookers are designed to accommodate temperatures of 210°F to 250°F, with some electric cookers able to manage up to 285°F.

Is it really true that a rice cooker can cook anything you could make over the stove? Well, almost. However miraculous, a home rice cooker can't do quite everything—you'll notice from the temperature specs that even the hottest rice cookers don't reach 300°F and aren't capable of high-temperature cooking. That's for safety reasons, among others, and it explains why you won't find recipes for roasts or deep-fried dishes in this book.

If you've recently purchased a brand-new rice cooker, we urge you to take a moment to read through the provided owners' manual. Most are concise and to the point and won't take long to read, and it's an important step in getting to know your rice cooker.

Types of Rice Cookers

The two most common types of rice cookers are the "On/Off" style and the "Keep Warm" version. In preparing basic rice, an On/Off cooker follows a preset timer and heating process that results in properly cooked rice. When it reaches the end of the cycle, the cooker turns itself off. This is the original, most traditional, and, if you can find one, usually the most affordable type of rice cooker—no frills, not even a Done light to signal that the rice is ready. These basic cookers do not normally offer non-stick pots or steamer units, but if you only want to cook rice, it will serve the purpose.

Unless your rice cooker is a family heirloom or something you found secondhand,

your model probably has at least one more function, and it's the one that unlocks the potential of the rice cooker as an invaluable cooking appliance.

"Keep Warm" Rice Cookers

The Keep Warm rice cooker achieves a high heat, then reduces the heat when the rice is done, maintaining it at a warm temperature. Most Keep Warm cookers sold today offer the ability to switch between the Cook and Keep Warm settings manually. This setting makes it possible to adjust and control the heating element beneath the cooking pot, and it was the introduction of this kind of rice cooker that unleashed the machine's full potential as an everyday cooking appliance with capabilities far beyond just cooking rice.

Most recipes in this book are prepared for Keep Warm cookers that allow manual switching between the Cook and Keep Warm settings. When a recipe says to turn your cooker to High, it refers to the Cook or On setting. Keep Warm is used for medium heat and to simmer.

A Note on Newer, High-End Rice Cookers

In recent years some enthusiastic foodies have become enraptured by new rice cooker technologies. Known as induction and fuzzy-logic cookers, these devices have taken rice-cooking automation to the next level of simplicity and consistency. These machines really do prepare something like the perfect pot of rice—but they also carry price tags to match, and are out of reach for most consumers. The trade-off with induction and fuzzy-logic rice cookers is that they are more or less just that: rice cookers. They don't allow for heat adjustment once the lid is closed, and in fact most don't operate at all with an open lid: few of these hi-tech machines can be used to prepare foods they weren't preprogrammed to cook, let alone complete meals.

Basic Rice Cooker Features

If you're new to the world of rice cookers, you'll want to experiment with and explore your new machine before diving into the recipes in this book. Let's start with a look at the basic dimensions, features, and principles of the On/Off/Warm rice cookers:

Rice Cooker Size

Rice cookers are measured by the maximum number of cups of rice they can produce at a time. The smallest cookers on the market today prepare about 3 cups of rice; the largest can cook up to about 24 cups at at time, and unless your household goes through a gallon and a half of rice, soup, or really anything else every couple of days, this is probably not the right machine for you. The recommended rice cooker size for a family of three to four is the 8-cup version, which can cook up to 10 cups of rice and allows enough real estate within the inner pot to do other cooking besides cooking rice.

The Pot

The home rice cooker was first introduced as an extremely simple contraption—a metal pot atop a heating element with a switch—and is still based on this same principle. The two biggest differences between the early machines of the 1950s and the ones in our homes today are temperature control and the range of materials from which pots are now made. That range is almost as wide as that stovetop pots and pans: anodized aluminum, nonstick, even ceramic and stainless steel pots have all become common. The aluminum models conduct the highest possible level of heat in a rice cooker, but the nonstick variety is by far the most popular because it makes cleanup a snap.

The Lid

Some rice cookers feature metal lids or covers; others use glass. The glass lids make it a bit easier to peek in on whatever's cooking, but only if you're the extremely disciplined type—most of us lift the lid to check on our dishes, and that's almost always okay. The notable exception here, of course, is when you're actually cooking rice itself, in which case you'll want to leave that cover in place until the rice is done!

Steamer Trays

Depending on your model, your rice cooker may have come with a steamer basket or perforated metal tray that sits above the pot to allow steaming while whatever's in the pot is cooking. Steaming can also be done independently of other cooking, by boiling water in an otherwise empty pot.

Warm Switch

The rice cooker automatically shifts to Warm when the thermostat reaches the cooker's preset temperature limit (usually 210°F to 250°F, or 100°C to 120°C). Most Keep Warm modes operate at 150°F or above, allowing them to safely keep rice warm overnight if not much longer. This switch is the key to easy rice cooker cooking because it allows you to adjust and control the cooking temperature yourself. For most dishes, you'll start with your rice cooker set to On or Cook. You'll switch the cooker manually to Warm when the recipe calls for simmering or medium heat.

Fuse Protector

Nothing is more important than safety when operating an appliance, especially an appliance like the rice cooker, which is often left unattended when it's making rice. All rice cookers sold today come with a fuse protector for automatic shutoff should the internal thermostat fail.

Where to Start?

Now that you have a better sense of how rice cookers work and what features are available on your own cooker, you're ready to start trying some of the 175 great recipes collected in this book.

You may have picked up *The "I Love My Rice Cooker" Recipe Book* because you saw a dish you just had to try—if so, why not go ahead and start there? If you're interested in rice cooker cooking and aren't sure where to start, flip through the recipes until you've found a dish similar to one you already know and love: there's no better way to begin than with a meal that makes you happy. From there you can branch out to all the other great dishes this book has to offer. Enjoy!

Essential Basics

This is where it all starts—whether you're brand-new to rice cookers, just got a new model, or simply haven't yet cooked anything but rice in yours, you'll learn a lot by trying a few of the following basic recipes. There's a pasta primer here; a warm, sustaining oatmeal recipe; and even a Japanese-style rice porridge. Unlike the recipes in the rest of this book, these first dishes don't share an essential ingredient or come to us from the same cuisine. What they have in common is that each of them is simple, easy to shop for, and straightforward to prepare. Rice, porridge, oats, and pasta are great dishes to start with, not only because they're easy but because for so many of us they're essential. You'll come back to them again and again as you begin to cook regularly with your rice cooker. For now let's get started with the most basic rice cooker dish of all.

Long-Grain White Rice

The standard measure for cooking long-grain white rice is three parts water to two parts rice, but many people also use the knuckle method—with the rice in the pot and your fingertip just touching the top of the rice, add water until it reaches your first knuckle.

Yields 3 cups cooked rice

1 cup long-grain white rice
1½ cups water

1 Rinse the rice in cold water, straining through a strainer or colander. Add the rice to the rice cooker pot.

2 Add the water. The water should cover the rice by about ½ inch. Cover and set to Cook.

3 When the rice cooker finishes cooking the rice, let it sit for about 5 minutes to vent off the remaining steam, then fluff before serving.

Brown Rice

All rice begins as brown rice, which has a thick bran exterior, making it difficult for moisture to penetrate all the way into the grain. When cooking brown rice you'll need to allow some extra time, and the proportions are slightly different, but the process remains the same.

Serves 2

1 cup brown rice
2 cups water

1 Rinse the rice in cold water, straining through a strainer or colander. Add the rice to the pot.

2 Add the water to the pot. Water should cover the rice by about ¾ inch. Cover and set to Cook.

3 When the rice cooker finishes cooking the rice, let it sit for about 5 minutes to vent off the remaining steam, then fluff before serving.

Sushi Rice

One of the best things about going out for sushi is the amazing quality of the rice served in most Japanese restaurants. Delicate, moist, and surprisingly flavorful, the artful thumb-sized portions make diners wonder, "Why doesn't my rice turn out like that?" Yes, it's partly the rice itself, but the final product is all in the preparation.

Yields 5 cups cooked rice

2 cups sushi rice
3 cups cold water
½ cup rice vinegar
¼ cup white sugar
1 teaspoon salt

1 Rinse the rice in cold water, straining through a strainer or colander. Add the rice to the rice cooker pot.

2 Add the water to the cooker pot. Water should cover the rice by about ¾ inch. Cover and set to Cook.

3 While the rice is cooking, prepare the vinegar mixture: In a small pan over medium heat, add the rice vinegar, sugar, and salt and mix well until the sugar dissolves. Pour the vinegar mixture into a small bowl and set aside to cool.

4 Spread the cooked rice into a large non-metallic plate or bowl. Sprinkle the vinegar mixture over the rice and fold it into the rice with a large serving spoon in a spiral pattern, starting from the outside. Be careful not to smash the rice. Continue until all of the vinegar is used.

Before Rolling Your Sushi

Before rolling your sushi, "fan" the rice by folding the rice frequently to cool it and remove moisture from the rice. This process gives sushi rice its signature sticky texture and glossy shine. When cooled, keep the rice at room temperature—not more than 2 hours—covered with a clean, damp towel. Don't refrigerate the rice, as it will harden.

Rice Congee

Congee isn't a well-known word in American cooking—yet. This simply satisfying porridge is wildly popular throughout Asia and is becoming more popular among in-the-know diners in larger US cities. As you'll see in Chapter 6, congee lends itself to lots of variations, from savory to sweet.

Serves 2

1 cup long-grain white rice
3 cups water

1 Rinse the rice in cold water, straining through a strainer or colander, and add the rice to the pot.

2 Add the water, cover, and set to Cook. When the pot begins to bubble over, stir and continue to cook partially covered for about 15 minutes or desired doneness is achieved.

Warm Oats

Fresh fruits and nuts add color and variety to this toasty breakfast dish. Bananas provide a bright finish to Warm Oats and don't require any cooking. The same goes for berries of almost any kind, but especially blueberries. For a nighttime treat try blackberries.

Serves 2

5 cups water or as needed
3 cups rolled oats
1 tablespoon honey

1 Add the water to the pot, cover, and set to Cook. When the water boils, stir in the oats and then the honey; stir to combine.

2 Cook for about 5 minutes until oats are cooked through. Add additional water if necessary to achieve desired consistency.

Pasta

It's often recommended to salt the water before cooking pasta, but what does that mean? Opinions vary—many cooks say the water should taste like the sea, but we recommend starting somewhere a little fresher than that, about 1 tablespoon per gallon of cooking water.

Serves 2

7 cups water
½ pound pasta
½ tablespoon salt

1 Add the water to the pot, cover, and set to Cook. When the water boils, add the pasta and salt; stir the pasta gently and frequently to prevent sticking.

2 Cover and cook for about 10 minutes or until desired doneness (cooking time varies depending on the type of pasta).

The "Sticky" Issue

If your pasta is sticky, do not add oil and stir it more. Oil will not prevent the pasta from sticking and in fact may have the undesired effect of coating the pasta, preventing it from combining well with your sauce. Pasta tends to stick together if it is not stirred during the critical first moments of cooking.

Chicken Stock

Some grocers and brands have begun to market "chicken bone stock" as a higher-end version of chicken stock, and it often is a step up as many store-bought stocks are made without bones. This homemade bone stock promises to be a step up from anything that comes in a box.

Yields 4 cups

5 cups cold water, or enough to immerse the chicken

2 pounds chicken parts (bones, back, necks)

1 (2-inch) piece fresh ginger, sliced

4 green onions, cut into finger-length pieces

¼ teaspoon salt

1 Add the water, chicken parts, ginger, and green onions to the pot. Cover and set to Cook.

2 When the water boils, switch the rice cooker to Warm and simmer for about 1 hour.

3 After 1 hour, uncover and skim the top of the stock. Add the salt, cover, and continue to simmer on Warm for another hour.

4 Remove and discard the solids. Strain the stock in a strainer or colander and refrigerate or freeze.

Pork Stock

This is a great bone stock, and even though this recipe calls for pork bones, you can add chicken or even beef bones to introduce more flavors. You can also make the different kinds of stock separately, then combine them to experiment with different tastes.

Yields 4 cups

5 cups cold water, or more as needed to immerse the pork bones

2 pounds pork bones

3 celery stalks, coarsely chopped

2 medium carrots, peeled and coarsely chopped into bite-sized cubes

1 onion, peeled and coarsely chopped

¼ teaspoon salt

1 Add the water, bones, celery, carrots, and onions to the pot. Cover the pot and set to Cook.

2 When the stock boils, switch the cooker to Warm and simmer for about 1 hour.

3 After 1 hour, skim the top of the stock. Add the salt, cover, and continue to simmer on Warm for another hour.

4 Remove and discard the solids. Strain the stock in a strainer or colander and refrigerate or freeze.

Shrimp Stock

When a recipe calls for a seafood stock, you really can't substitute it with something else—most don't turn out quite right when a chicken or beef base is used instead. Making fish stock isn't for everyone, so if you're among those who'd rather keep it simple, try this Shrimp Stock anywhere fish stock is called for.

Yields 3 cups

1 tablespoon vegetable oil

1 tablespoon finely chopped pancetta

Heads, shells, and tails from 2 pounds shrimp (see note)

4 cups water

1   Add the oil to the pot, cover, and set to Cook. When the base of the pot gets warm add the pancetta and cook for 1–2 minutes until fragrant.

2   Add the shrimp parts and cook for about 3 minutes more, covered and stirring occasionally. Add the water, cover, and allow the stock to come to a boil.

3   Switch to Warm and simmer covered about 30 minutes. Remove and discard the solids. Strain the stock in a strainer or colander and refrigerate or freeze.

Save Up for Shrimp Stock

Whenever you eat shrimp, remember to save (and freeze) the leftover shells in small batches (sealed in airtight containers or bags). A family of two typically takes at least 2 months to accumulate enough leftover shrimp shells to make 3 cups of stock!

Vegetable Stock

This stock is great when preparing vegetarian dishes and for dishes that would be overpowered by the strong flavors of meat-based stocks. It's as universal as cooking stocks come, so double up the recipe and freeze what you don't use—it'll keep in the freezer for up to 6 months.

Yields 3 cups

4 cups cold water, or more as needed to immerse the vegetables

3 celery stalks, stems coarsely chopped, retaining leaves

1 medium onion, peeled and sliced

2 medium carrots, peeled and coarsely chopped into cubes

2 bay leaves

¼ teaspoon salt

1   Add the water to the pot, cover, and set to Cook. When the water boils, add all the ingredients except the salt. Cover pot and return to a boil.

2   Switch to Warm, add the salt, cover, and simmer for about 1 hour.

3   Remove and discard the solids. Strain the stock in a strainer or colander and refrigerate or freeze.

Soybean Stock

Plain boiled soybeans are amazingly delicious and nutritious, and if you salt the water as described in the following instructions, you have the popular Japanese appetizer edamame. The leftover cooking liquid is what we're really after here; it is a great alternative to vegetable stock.

Yields 4 cups

5 cups water
½ pound dried soybeans, soaked in water overnight, drained, and rinsed before using
1 teaspoon salt

1 Add the water to the pot, cover, and set to Cook. When the water boils, add the soybeans, cover, and boil for 30 minutes, stirring occasionally and skimming off the foam from the top of the water.

2 Switch to Warm and simmer for about 1 hour.

3 Stir in the salt. Remove and discard the solids, or save the soybeans to eat as a snack. Strain the stock in a strainer or colander and refrigerate or freeze.

Bean Soaking Methods

Soaking the dried soybeans shortens the cooking time and improves their flavor and texture. Let the soybeans soak in water (about 5 cups water per ½ pound beans) at room temperature for 6–8 hours or overnight. Before cooking, drain and rinse the beans. Or, to accelerate the soaking process, cook the soybeans in boiling water (about 5 cups water per ½ pound beans) for 5 minutes, then allow the beans to soak in cooking water for 1 hour. Before proceeding with the recipe, drain and rinse the beans.

3

Appetizers

If sharing is caring, then this chapter is bursting with love. These finger foods and appetizers boast the magical ability to bring people together—a group of friends and family at your next holiday party, a Super Bowl gathering, or just a great Friday night around the table. Even better, the rice cooker allows hands-free cooking, which permits you more time to socialize with your guests without heating up the house. Plus, cooking with steam allows moisture into the food and traps the spices while the food slow cooks. From Salmon Patties and Garlic Mushrooms to Stuffed Tomatoes and Toasted Pita Pizza, the hardest decision you'll have to make is which one to serve first!

Tuna and Cheese Patties

Fish and cheese aren't often found paired together, even in parts of the world where both are abundant. Tuna is an exception; its natural oils and texture pair well with a variety of cheeses, including mozzarella, as in these light yet savory patties.

Serves 4

- 2 tablespoons butter
- ¼ cup flour
- ¼ teaspoon salt
- ½ cup whole milk
- 1 (6-ounce) can tuna in water, flaked
- 3 ounces shredded mozzarella
- 1 large egg, lightly whisked
- ½ cup finely chopped fresh cilantro
- 3 tablespoons olive oil

1 Add the butter to the pot, cover, and set to Cook. When the butter has melted, add the flour and salt, mixing well.

2 Stir in the milk slowly until mixture thickens.

3 Add the tuna and the cheese and mix well until cheese melts. Switch to Off.

4 When cool enough to handle, slowly stir the egg into the mixture, then add the cilantro. Mix well, form into 4 equal-sized patties, and chill in the refrigerator for 30 minutes.

5 While patties are chilling, clean out the pot and wipe dry. Add the oil and set to Cook. When the oil is hot, cook the patties covered about 4 minutes per side or until golden brown.

Mini Fish Kebabs

Elsewhere in the world, "kebab" refers not to skewers but to many different ways of serving grilled meats. In the US it is almost always used interchangeably with "shish kebab," as it is here in these spicy, lime-splashed treats.

Yields 12 mini skewers

- 2 whole cloves garlic, peeled and crushed
- 2 teaspoons grated ginger
- ½ teaspoon turmeric
- 1 teaspoon fish sauce
- 2 tablespoons lime juice
- 1 teaspoon brown sugar
- ¼ teaspoon red pepper flakes
- 3 tablespoons extra-virgin olive oil
- 2 (8-ounce) threadfin or snapper fillets, cut into 1-inch cubes
- 1 tablespoon vegetable oil
- 1 lime, cut into wedges

1 In a medium bowl, add the garlic, ginger, turmeric, fish sauce, lime juice, brown sugar, red pepper flakes, and olive oil and stir to combine. Add the fish and marinate for 10–15 minutes in the refrigerator.

2 Thread 2 or 3 cubes of fish onto skewers about 4 inches in length or as needed to fit into your rice cooker.

3 Add the vegetable oil to the pot, cover, and set to Cook. When the base gets warm, add the skewers and cook covered about 5 minutes. Flip the skewers and cook for 5 minutes more.

4 Transfer the skewers to a serving platter and serve with lime wedges.

Fish Salad

Lettuce and cucumber tend to contain a lot of water and may make the entire salad too wet. To avoid this, drain the excess liquid, including from the steamed fish, while preparing the ingredients.

Serves 4

4 cups water

2 (8-ounce) snapper, salmon, or mackerel fillets

2 tablespoons plus 2 teaspoons chopped fresh mint

2 tablespoons plus 2 teaspoons chopped fresh basil

2 tablespoons plus 2 teaspoons chopped fresh cilantro

6 lettuce leaves, finely sliced

1 medium shallot, peeled and thinly sliced

1 small cucumber, peeled and sliced

1 Add the water to the pot, cover, and set to Cook. While the water is heating, arrange the fish on a plate that will fit in your rice cooker's steamer basket or insert.

2 When the water boils, place the fish in the pot, cover, and steam until cooked through, about 7 minutes.

3 Remove fish and set aside. Once cool, break the fish into bite-sized flakes. Drain any excess liquid.

4 In a small bowl, combine mint, basil, and cilantro.

5 In a medium bowl, toss the fish flakes with the lettuce, shallots, and herb medley and top with the cucumber.

A Dressing for Fish Salad

Combine 1 tablespoon fish sauce, 2 tablespoons lemon juice, ½ teaspoon sugar, and the finely chopped white part of 1 lemongrass stalk in a small bowl and whisk to combine. Drizzle this light and tangy dressing over Fish Salad before serving.

Salmon Patties

When the historic Lewis and Clark expedition finally reached what is now the Columbia River in the Pacific Northwest, it's said the men nearly starved to death despite being in the heart of the world's greatest salmon fishery. Luckily, we know better.

Yields 4 patties

1 large egg, lightly whisked
2 (6-ounce) cans salmon, flaked
¼ cup finely chopped fresh cilantro,
¼ teaspoon salt
¼ teaspoon ground black pepper
2 tablespoons vegetable oil
4 small lemon wedges

1 In a medium bowl, add half of the whisked egg and the salmon and stir to combine. Add the cilantro, salt, pepper, and remaining egg and mix until the egg is completely absorbed into the salmon. Form the mixture into 4 flat patties.

2 Add the oil to the pot, cover, and set to Cook. When the pot warms, add the patties and cook covered until golden brown and slightly crisp, about 3 minutes per side.

3 Serve with a squeeze of lemon.

Serving Suggestion

If you want your serving dish to look as amazing as these Salmon Patties taste, try presenting these patties to your guests atop a bed of thinly sliced lemon and 2 tablespoons of fresh parsley leaves.

Bacon, Onion, and Potato Hash

To "hash" means to chop food into small pieces, thus hashed browns, the American breakfast classic. This Bacon, Onion, and Potato Hash is a timeless standard, and a great way to use extra meat and potatoes.

Serves 2

4 cups water

2 medium Yukon gold potatoes, whole and unpeeled

1 tablespoon extra-virgin olive oil

1 medium onion, peeled and thinly sliced

4 slices bacon, roughly chopped

1 clove garlic, peeled and finely minced

¼ teaspoon salt

¼ teaspoon ground black pepper

1 Add the water to the pot, cover, and set to Cook.

2 When the water boils, add the potatoes. If necessary, add enough water to cover the potatoes, then return to a boil. Cover and cook about 10 minutes.

3 Remove the potatoes, peeling and cubing them once cool enough to handle. Set aside.

4 Clean out the pot and wipe it dry. Add the oil to the pot, cover, and set to Cook. When the base gets warm, add the onions and cook about 5 minutes until translucent and slightly tender.

5 Add the potato cubes, cover, and cook for about 3 minutes.

6 Add the bacon, garlic, salt, and pepper. Cover and cook for about 5 minutes, stirring occasionally until potatoes are golden and fork-tender.

Potato, Bell Pepper, and Mushroom Hash

Vegetarians hash it out just as well as the carnivores do. When preparing vegetables in a hash like this one, a good rule of thumb is to add them in order of their firmness, from most to least.

Serves 2

- 4 cups water
- 2 medium russet potatoes, whole and unpeeled
- 1 tablespoon extra-virgin olive oil
- 1 medium onion, peeled and thinly sliced
- ½ medium green bell pepper, seeded and sliced
- ½ medium red bell pepper, seeded and sliced
- 6 white mushrooms, sliced
- 1 egg, lightly whisked
- ¼ teaspoon salt
- ¼ teaspoon ground black pepper

1 Add the water to the pot, cover, and set to Cook.

2 When the water boils, add the potatoes. If necessary, add enough water to cover the potatoes, then return to a boil. Cover and cook about 10 minutes.

3 Remove the potatoes, peeling and cubing them once cool enough to handle. Set aside.

4 Clean out the pot and wipe it dry. Add the oil to the pot, cover, and set to Cook. When the base gets warm, add the onions and cook about 5 minutes until translucent and slightly tender.

5 Add the potato cubes, cover, and cook for about 3 minutes.

6 Add the bell peppers, mushrooms, egg, salt, and black pepper. Cook covered about 5 minutes, stirring several times to scramble the egg into smaller pieces. Remove promptly when potatoes are golden and fork-tender.

Potato Tips

Potatoes are sometimes grouped into starchy, medium, and waxy. Starchy potato varieties, such as russets, are great for cooking—they break up just a bit during cooking and absorb flavors better than the waxier varieties like white or red potatoes.

Mashed Sweet Potatoes

Sweet potatoes are native to the Americas and are only distantly related to the common potato. In fact, both plant families acquired the name from Spanish explorers in the Americas, who blended various native words for all kinds of round tubers to come up with "patata."

Serves 3

4 cups water

2 medium sweet potatoes, peeled and cut into 2-inch chunks

2 tablespoons butter

1 tablespoon brown sugar

½ cup whole milk

¼ teaspoon salt

¼ teaspoon ground black pepper

1 Add the water to the pot, cover, and set to Cook. While the water is heating, place the sweet potatoes on a plate that will fit in your rice cooker's steamer basket or insert.

2 When the water boils, place the sweet potatoes in the pot, cover, and steam until cooked through, about 15 minutes. Remove and set aside in a large bowl.

3 Clean out the pot and wipe dry, cover, and set to Cook. Add the butter and sugar and allow to melt, then slowly stir in the milk.

4 When the mixture begins to boil, stir well and switch cooker to Off.

5 Ladle the mixture into the sweet potatoes and mash until smooth. Season with the salt and pepper. Serve warm.

Mini Ham and Corn Omelets

If you don't have time to work in batches to create individual mini omelets, create a regular-sized omelet and then use a cookie cutter to cut out presentable bite-sized appetizer omelets.

Serves 4

3 slices deli ham, finely diced

2 cup fresh corn kernels

2 tablespoons finely chopped green onions

2 large eggs, lightly whisked

¼ teaspoon salt

¼ teaspoon ground black pepper

3 tablespoons vegetable oil

1 In a medium bowl, add the ham, corn kernels, and green onions and stir to mix. Add the whisked egg, stirring to combine well. Season with the salt and pepper.

2 Add half the oil to the rice cooker, cover, and set to Cook. When the base gets warm, add half the egg mixture in 2-tablespoon circles across the base of the pot. Cook covered about 2 minutes per side until the edges turn brown and crisp. Repeat with remaining oil and egg mixture. Serve warm.

Hotshot Sweet Corn

Add Szechuan peppercorns for a spicy, maybe even tongue-numbing, kick. You can also use cooked corn on the cob for this recipe: just before serving, slather the buttered green onion–chili mix onto the corn on the cob. And, once this corn is ready to go, serve on warm toasted bread or with Long-Grain White Rice (see Chapter 2).

Serves 4

½ tablespoon butter

4 green onions, finely chopped

1 teaspoon red pepper flakes

1 teaspoon ground black pepper

¼ teaspoon salt

½ teaspoon brown sugar

1 (15-ounce) can whole kernel corn kernels, drained

1 Add the butter to the pot, cover, and set to Cook.

2 When the base of the pot gets warm, add the green onions, red pepper flakes, black pepper, salt, brown sugar, and corn kernels; cook for 2 minutes. Stir well, cover, and cook for 2 minutes more. Serve warm.

Stuffed Tomatoes

Give this recipe a try with beefsteak red tomatoes—they tend to run pretty big and are more forgiving as a result. Once you have this recipe down, you've opened the world of what in Mexican cuisine is called a *relleno*, or "stuffed" produce. Try green tomatoes, or for a classic Mexican treat use a big green bell pepper.

Serves 4

- 2 tablespoons extra-virgin olive oil
- 1 medium onion, peeled and diced
- 2 cloves garlic, peeled and minced
- 1 teaspoon grated ginger
- ¼ teaspoon ground black pepper
- 1 teaspoon curry powder
- ½ pound ground beef
- 3 tablespoons water
- 1 poblano, seeded and thinly sliced
- 1 tablespoon chopped fresh cilantro
- 4 large tomatoes
- 2 tablespoons fresh parsley leaves

1 Add the oil to the pot, cover, and set to Warm. When the base gets hot, add the onions and cook for about 2 minutes or until translucent and slightly tender.

2 Add the garlic, ginger, black pepper, and curry power and cook for about 2 minutes.

3 Add the ground beef to the pot and break up into small bits; cook for about 3 more minutes or until the beef is browned all over.

4 Add the water, mix well, cover, and cook for 8 minutes. When the mixture begins to bubble vigorously, switch the cooker to Warm and cook covered until beef is done, about 7 more minutes.

5 Switch to Cook, add the poblano pepper and cilantro, and cook uncovered for about 2 minutes, stirring occasionally.

6 Cut the top off of each tomato and scoop out the flesh. Spoon the beef mixture into the tomatoes, garnish with parsley, and serve hot.

Garlic Mushrooms

Spoon these mushrooms over warm toasted bread to serve. For a more garlicky flavor, you can rub crushed garlic directly on the toast. Drown it in butter before topping with the mushrooms for a decadent dinner starter.

Serves 2

- 2 tablespoons butter, divided
- 2 cloves garlic, peeled and crushed whole
- ½ pound mushrooms, sliced
- 1 teaspoon finely chopped fresh parsley
- ¼ teaspoon salt
- ¼ teaspoon ground black pepper

1 Add 1 tablespoon of the butter to the pot and set to Cook. When the base gets warm, add the garlic and cook about 3 minutes until fragrant.

2 Add the mushrooms and cook for 5 minutes. Stir in the remaining tablespoon of butter and continue to cook, stirring occasionally. If the mushrooms seem to be cooking too quickly, switch to Warm. Cook until mushrooms turn completely soft.

3 Add the parsley, salt, and pepper. Mix well and serve warm.

Toasted Almonds

Any toasted nuts can be prepared this way—it's like pan-popped corn, without the oil. Once toasted, the almonds (or cashews, walnuts, etc.) make a great snack and a fantastic garnish for all kinds of dishes.

Serves 4

- 3 cups slivered raw almonds

Cover rice cooker and set to Cook. When the base of the pot gets warm, add the almonds and stir until golden brown.

Toasting Nuts

When you need to toast nuts as part of a larger dish, do it before you start any other cooking; it will save you time and possible headaches later on in the process when your pot is full or needs a cleaning and the rest of your dish is ready.

Toasted Pita Pizza

No, it's not gluten-free pizza, but there are plenty of places to get that these days. Surprisingly substantial, this is a great appetizer to serve when you know your guests may be hungry on arrival, either because you're serving a late dinner or because you'll be in the kitchen for a while.

Serves 2

4 slices pita bread

4 slices deli ham, chopped and divided

1 cup finely cubed pineapple, divided

½ cup grated Cheddar cheese, divided

½ cup grated mozzarella cheese, divided

1 Cover the rice cooker and set to Cook. When the base warms, add one pita and sprinkle with a quarter of the ham and pineapple. Cover and cook about 4 minutes.

2 Add a quarter of each cheese, cover, and cook about 5 minutes more until cheese is melted. Repeat with the remaining pitas and serve hot.

4

Soups

Soups nourish and warm us in every way. They remind of us our mothers, cold nights by the fireplace, and even televised sporting events in a room full of friends. Over the millennia, soups have been believed to help heal us when we're sick. They help us lose weight by satisfying our appetites, and even save us money on our weekly grocery budgets. The rice cooker is the one-pot wonder you easily can use to create tasty soups based on flavors from around the world. Soups are also a great vehicle to get some of those stubborn family members to eat their veggies. And if prepping vegetables isn't fun for you or you are strapped for time, most grocers provide precut versions in not only the produce section but also the freezer section. From Kimchi Tofu Soup and Cream of Mushroom Soup to Southern Corn Chowder, look to the soups in this chapter for a nutrient-rich, filling, and complete comfort meal.

Cabbage and Tomato Soup

Cabbage has been essential to European cuisine for at least a thousand years, but almost half the global crop now grows in China. Cabbage and Tomato Soup is a great source of B-complex vitamins and especially vitamin C, and a healthy amount of dietary fiber.

Serves 4

4 cups water, divided

1 small (12–16-ounce) head cabbage, thinly sliced

½ (14½-ounce) can diced tomatoes with juice

¼ teaspoon salt

¼ teaspoon ground black pepper

½ teaspoon dried oregano, for garnish

1   Add 2 cups of the water to the pot, cover, and set to Cook. When the water boils, add the cabbage and the tomatoes, stir, and continue to cook for about 5 minutes.

2   Add the remaining 2 cups water. Once it returns to a boil, cover and simmer about 15 minutes or until the cabbage is tender.

3   Add the salt and pepper. Garnish with oregano and serve warm.

Love That Lycopene

Tomatoes are one of the best sources of lycopene, a powerful antioxidant that maintains and supports healthy cells. Lycopene can only be dissolved in oils, so lightly sauté your tomatoes in oil to get all the nutrients they have to offer.

Spinach Soup with Pork Meatballs

Unless you're looking for that old canned flavor, always be careful not to overcook spinach. As in this recipe, spinach should almost always be the last vegetable added to a soup, stir-fry, or other high-heat dish, as it wilts and loses flavor very quickly under heat.

Serves 4

- ½ pound ground pork
- ½ teaspoon salt, divided
- ½ teaspoon ground white pepper, divided
- ¼ teaspoon sesame oil
- ¼ tablespoon corn flour
- 4 cups water
- 4 fresh shiitake mushroom caps, thinly sliced
- 3 tightly packed cups fresh baby spinach
- 1 (10½-ounce) pack soft tofu, cut into ½-inch cubes

1. In a medium bowl, combine the ground pork, ¼ teaspoon salt, ¼ teaspoon pepper, sesame oil, and corn flour and stir to mix. Set aside.

2. Add the water to the pot, cover, and set to Cook. When the water boils, form the pork mixture into marble-sized balls and add to the pot.

3. Add the mushrooms and boil covered for 15 minutes.

4. Switch to Warm and cook 15 minutes more. Add ¼ teaspoon salt and ¼ teaspoon pepper, stir in the spinach and tofu, and simmer covered for about 5 minutes. Serve warm.

Bean Sprouts and Tomato Soup

Bean sprouts are also known as mung bean sprouts and are a great source of vitamins, minerals, and amino acids. Coupled with the tomatoes, this is one nutrient-packed soup, and it's great any time of year.

Serves 4

1 tablespoon extra-virgin olive oil

½ cup lean pork, thinly sliced

1 medium fresh tomato, diced

4 cups water

3 cups bean sprouts

¼ teaspoon salt

¼ teaspoon ground white pepper

1 Add the oil to the pot, cover, and set to Cook. When the base gets warm, add the pork and cook covered for about 2 minutes.

2 Add the tomatoes and cook covered for 2 more minutes.

3 Add the water. When the soup starts to boil vigorously, switch the cooker to Warm and add the bean sprouts, salt, and pepper; allow the soup to simmer for about 10 minutes, stirring occasionally. Serve warm.

Kimchi Tofu Soup

Kimchi, a staple in South Korea, has become wildly popular in other countries in Asia and in Europe and North America. You can use kimchi as a key element in stir-fries, as a replacement for salsa with guacamole and chips, or as a flavor enhancer and base for soup, as in this recipe.

Serves 4

4 cups water

1 (10½-ounce) block soft tofu, cut into cubes

½ cup finely chopped kimchi

2 green onions, finely chopped, for garnish

1 Add the water to the pot, cover, and set to Cook. When the water boils, add the tofu, cover the rice cooker, and allow it to come to a simmer.

2 Switch the rice cooker to Warm, stir in the kimchi, and simmer covered for 5 minutes. Garnish with the green onions and serve.

Halibut-Asparagus Soup with Pancetta

Pancetta releases oil as it cooks, which in this soup preparation is used to cook the asparagus. The pancetta oil brings a robustness to the soup and balances the flavor in a way you'll miss if you cook the asparagus in vegetable oil.

Serves 2

1 tablespoon finely diced pancetta

4 ounces (¼ pound) fresh asparagus, cut into finger-length pieces

3 cups water (or use half water and half chicken stock)

2 (8-ounce) halibut fillets, cut into ½-inch slices

¼ teaspoon salt

¼ teaspoon ground white pepper

1 green onion, finely chopped, for garnish

1 teaspoon seeded and thinly sliced red chili pepper, for garnish

1 Cover the pot and set to Cook. When the base warms, add the pancetta and cook until brown at the edges and oily, about 3 minutes.

2 Add the asparagus and cook until light in color and tender, about 8 minutes. Divide the mixture between the serving bowls.

3 Wipe the oil from the pot, add the water, cover, and set to Cook. When the water comes to a boil, add the fish and cook about 6 minutes or until opaque. Remove the fish and distribute among your bowls.

4 Ladle soup into serving bowls. Add the salt and white pepper. Garnish with the green onion and red chili and serve hot.

Minestrone

Minestrone might be the most quintessential of Italian soups. The common ingredients in minestrone include onions, celery, carrots, beans, and tomatoes. You can of course vary the thickness of yours by adjusting the amount of liquid.

Serves 4

- 2 tablespoons extra-virgin olive oil
- 2 cloves garlic, peeled and finely minced
- 1 medium onion, peeled and thinly sliced
- 1 medium potato, peeled and diced
- 1 small carrot, peeled and diced
- 2 celery stalks, diced
- 8 cherry tomatoes, halved
- 3 cups water
- 3 cups Vegetable Stock (see Chapter 2)
- ½ cup uncooked shell pasta
- ¼ teaspoon salt
- ¼ teaspoon ground black pepper
- ½ teaspoon dried basil, for garnish

1 Add the oil to the rice cooker, cover, and set to Cook. When the base gets warm, add the garlic and onion and cook for about 3 minutes.

2 Add the potatoes, carrots, celery, and tomatoes and cook for another 2 minutes.

3 Add the water and stock, cover, and bring to a boil.

4 When the potatoes are fork-tender, add the pasta and boil for another 6 minutes or until pasta is cooked to taste.

5 Switch to Warm and simmer covered for about 15 minutes.

6 Add the salt and pepper, garnish with the basil, and serve warm.

Cream of Mushroom Soup

There are endless variations to most classic soups, and the varieties of cream of mushroom soup range from the simplest, near-stock style to decadent truffle oil concoctions. This accessible preparation is a great starting point for your own explorations.

Serves 4

½ pound cremini mushrooms
2 tablespoons butter, divided
½ medium onion, peeled and finely chopped
3 cups Vegetable Stock (see Chapter 2)
¼ teaspoon salt
¼ teaspoon ground black pepper
1 cup heavy cream

1 Coarsely chop mushrooms in a food processor or with a sharp knife.

2 Add 1 tablespoon of the butter to the rice cooker, cover, and set to Cook. When the base of the pot warms and the butter melts, add the onions and cook for 5 minutes until onions become translucent and soft.

3 Add the mushrooms and remaining butter and continue to cook covered for 5–7 minutes, stirring often, until the mushrooms soften.

4 Slowly stir in the stock and salt and pepper, cover the rice cooker, and bring to a boil.

5 Switch the rice cooker to Warm, stir in the heavy cream slowly, and simmer covered for about 5 minutes. Serve warm.

Potato, Cabbage, and Spicy Sausage Soup

Compared to other soups in this chapter, such as Minestrone and Curried Carrot and Ginger Soup, this soup is very hearty thanks to the addition of the potato and meat. Substitute the sausage with chorizo or salami according to your own taste.

Serves 2

1 tablespoon extra-virgin olive oil

2 medium shallots, peeled and thinly sliced

2 cloves garlic, peeled and finely minced

2 spicy Italian sausages, cut into ½-inch-thick slices

1 medium potato, peeled and cut into ½-inch cubes

3 tightly packed cups finely shredded cabbage

4 cups Chicken or Vegetable Stock (see Chapter 2)

¼ teaspoon paprika, for garnish

1 Add the oil to the pot, cover, and set to Cook. When the pot is warm, add the shallots, garlic, and sausage. Cook for about 8 minutes until the onions are soft and the sausage browns at the edges.

2 Add the potatoes and cabbage and cook covered about 8 more minutes or until the cabbage is slightly tender, stirring frequently.

3 Add the stock, cover, and bring to a boil.

4 Switch to Warm. Simmer for about 25 minutes until potatoes are cooked through. Garnish with paprika and serve warm.

Vegetable Soup with Pinto Beans

The pinto is the most popular bean in both the United States and Mexico, and it is very popular in Brazil as well. This soup presents the pinto in a different light than Americans often see it, highlighting its soft, almost silky texture. If you'd like, top this soup with parsley leaves to add even more color.

Serves 4

2 medium tomatoes, diced

1 small eggplant, diced

1 medium carrot, peeled and diced

1 medium leek, cleaned thoroughly and very thinly sliced

1 (15-ounce) can pinto beans, drained, gently rinsed with water, then drained again

3 cups Vegetable Stock (see Chapter 2)

1 teaspoon dried parsley

1 Add all ingredients except the parsley to the pot. Cover, set to Cook, and bring to a boil.

2 Once boiling, switch to Warm and continue to simmer for 20 minutes or until vegetables become tender.

3 Add parsley and stir well. Serve warm.

Mushroom and Barley Soup

Try to use at least two if not all three listed varieties of mushrooms to increase the depth of earthy flavors in this dish. If your grocer is out of any of these, see if there's another variety in stock, the earthier and more unusual the better!

Serves 2

- 4 cups water
- 2 ounces washed and cleaned pearl barley, soaked at least 4 hours
- 1 tablespoon extra-virgin olive oil
- 3 medium shallots, peeled and thinly sliced
- 4 fresh shiitake mushroom caps, thinly sliced
- 6 white mushroom caps, thinly sliced
- 6 brown mushroom caps, thinly sliced
- ½ tablespoon butter
- 2 cups Vegetable Stock (see Chapter 2)
- 1 bay leaf
- ¼ teaspoon salt
- ¼ teaspoon ground black pepper
- ½ teaspoon dried oregano, for garnish

1 Add the water to the pot, cover, and set to Cook. When the water boils, add the barley, cover, and boil for 25 minutes or until barley softens. Strain the barley, reserving 2 cups of the cooking water. Set cooking water and barley aside.

2 Clean and wipe the pot dry. Add the oil to the pot, cover, and set to Cook. When the base is warm, add the shallots and cook about 3 minutes or until shallots soften.

3 Add the mushrooms and sauté for about 5 minutes or until tender.

4 Add the butter to the mushrooms and mix well. Add the barley and the reserved cooking water, the stock, bay leaf, and salt and pepper. Mix well and allow to come to a boil covered.

5 Switch cooker to Warm and simmer covered for about 20 minutes.

6 Remove bay leaf, garnish with oregano, and serve.

Ham-Bone Split Pea Soup

This soup will warm your insides during the winter months and your spirit any time of year. Round it out with a light merlot and some soul-soothing music for the full experience. If you don't have a fireplace, well, there's an app for that.

Serves 4

- 3 tablespoons butter
- 2 medium carrots, peeled and diced
- 2 celery stalks, diced
- 1 small onion, peeled and diced
- 1 (½-pound) hog jowl or ham bone
- 1 cup split green peas
- 4 cups Chicken Stock (see Chapter 2)
- 1 cup water
- 1 tablespoon cooking sherry
- 1 tablespoon dried thyme
- 1 teaspoon salt
- 1 teaspoon ground black pepper
- 4 tablespoons sour cream

1. Add the butter to the pot and set to Cook. When the pot gets warm, add the carrots, celery, and onion and cook about 3 minutes until the onions are translucent. Add the ham, peas, stock, water, sherry, thyme, salt, and pepper and cover.

2. When the soup starts to boil vigorously, switch the cooker to Warm and allow the soup to simmer covered for 10 minutes.

3. Transfer the ham to a cutting board. When it's cool enough to work with, remove any bone or thick fatty pieces and discard. Dice the remaining ham and add it back to the soup. Ladle into serving bowls and top each with 1 tablespoon of sour cream.

Curried Carrot and Ginger Soup

The curry powder makes this a mildly spicy soup, comforting on cold winter days. For a bigger kick, double both the ginger and the curry powder; preparing the soup this way also brings it a bit closer to its Indian roots.

Serves 2

- 1 tablespoon extra-virgin olive oil
- ½ medium onion, peeled and finely chopped
- 2 cloves garlic, peeled and finely minced
- 1 medium carrot, peeled and thinly sliced
- 1 teaspoon grated ginger
- ½ teaspoon curry powder
- 2 cups water
- ¼ teaspoon salt
- ¼ teaspoon ground black pepper
- 1 (½-inch) piece fresh ginger, shredded
- 1 cup coconut milk

1 Add the oil to the pot, cover, and set to Cook. When the pot is warm, add the onions and the garlic and cook until the onions are translucent, about 5 minutes.

2 Add the carrots, grated ginger, and curry powder and cook for about 3 minutes.

3 Add the water, cover, and bring to a boil.

4 Switch the cooker to Warm. Add the salt and pepper and the ginger shreds. Gently stir in the coconut milk and simmer covered for about 15 minutes. Serve warm.

Southern Corn Chowder

The can of cream-style corn in this recipe allows you to use less heavy cream and still end up with a smooth, silky base, and the bacon provides a depth and richness. The fresh thyme finishes the dish perfectly.

Serves 4

- 3 slices bacon, diced
- 3 tablespoons butter
- 1 small sweet onion, peeled and diced
- 1 large carrot, peeled and diced
- 2 celery stalks, diced
- 2 small russet potatoes, cut into ¼-inch cubes
- ⅛ teaspoon cayenne pepper
- 1 teaspoon salt
- 1 teaspoon ground black pepper
- 1 (15-ounce) can sweet corn, drained
- 1 (8¼-ounce) can cream-style sweet corn
- 4 cups Chicken Stock (see Chapter 2)
- 1 cup heavy cream
- 4 sprigs fresh thyme

1 Add the bacon to the pot, cover, and set to Cook. When the pot gets warm and the bacon starts crackling, remove the lid and stir while cooking about 3 minutes until the bacon is almost crisp. Add the butter, onion, carrot, and celery. Cook for an additional 2 minutes until onions are tender.

2 Add the potatoes, cayenne, salt, black pepper, sweet corn, cream-style corn, and stock and cover.

3 When the soup starts to boil vigorously, switch the rice cooker to Warm and allow the soup to simmer covered for 10 minutes. Turn the cooker to Off. Whisk in the heavy cream, add the thyme, and serve immediately.

Rice Dishes

It wouldn't be a rice cooker recipe book without a chapter on rice! Eaten around the world with different spices, preparations, and so many varieties, rice is the most popular cereal grain of all. Preparing rice the old-fashioned way takes a certain precision—you have to ensure that the precious little grains are nice and fluffy and cooked enough but not so overcooked that they become burnt. The rice cooker takes all that fuss away and does the trick automatically. This chapter includes recipes that incorporate a variety of proteins and different cuisines—from Shrimp Pilaf and Fragrant Coconut Rice to Bibimbap and Indian Vegetable Biryani—that highlight some of the various ways you can showcase this grain.

Seafood Tom Yum Rice

This easy fried-rice recipe—your household will come to know it by the scent of the herbs—makes use of tom yum paste, which is widely available in US supermarkets.

Serves 2

2 tablespoons vegetable oil

12 medium shrimp, peeled, deveined, and diced

1 lemongrass stalk, finely chopped (white part only)

2 teaspoons tom yum paste

1 cup chopped string beans

½ cup frozen corn

½ cup frozen green peas

½ cup diced green and red bell peppers

2 small red chili peppers, thinly sliced

3 tablespoons water

4 cups cooked Long-Grain White Rice (see Chapter 2)

1 Add the oil to the pot, cover, and set to Cook. When the base of the pot gets warm, add the shrimp and cook for 3 minutes or until pink. Remove the shrimp with a slotted spoon and set aside, leaving the remaining oil in the pot.

2 Add the lemongrass and cook until fragrant, about 3 minutes. Add the tom yum paste, beans, corn, peas, bell peppers, and red chili peppers. Cook for about 5 minutes.

3 Gradually stir in the water, cover, and wait for the mixture to reach a simmer. Uncover and continue cooking until the vegetables are tender, about 6 minutes.

4 Set to Warm. Return the shrimp to the pot and add the rice. Mix well. Keep the rice cooker on Warm until ready to serve.

Did You Know?

Lemongrass is also known as citronella grass or fever grass. Citronella oil is commonly used as a mosquito repellent.

Donburi Chicken Bowl

The Japanese words *donburi* and *don* are used interchangeably these days to mean "bowl of a meal of rice" or "bowl." The most common donburi in North American restaurants are katsudon (pork cutlet donburi), gyudon (beef donburi), oyakodon (chicken donburi), and unadon (eel donburi).

Serves 2

½ cup dashi stock

1 teaspoon mirin

1 teaspoon low-sodium soy sauce

¼ teaspoon salt

1 medium onion, peeled and thinly sliced, divided

1 boneless chicken thigh, cut into bite-sized pieces, divided

2 large eggs, lightly whisked, divided

4 cups warm cooked Sushi Rice (see Chapter 2) without the vinegar, divided into 2 serving bowls

1 In a medium bowl, mix the dashi stock, mirin, soy sauce, and salt. Add half of this mixture to the pot, cover, and set to Cook.

2 When the mixture reaches a simmer, add half of the onions and cook covered for about 3 minutes until the onions soften; switch to Warm if the mixture boils too vigorously.

3 Add half of the chicken, set the cooker to Cook, and stir-fry until cooked through, at least 5 minutes.

4 Switch the cooker to Warm and slowly pour in half of the eggs. Allow to simmer until the egg almost sets. Gently slide the chicken mixture into one of the bowls over the cooked rice.

5 Repeat with the remaining ingredients.

What Is Dashi Stock?

The two essential ingredients to dashi stock are kombu seaweed and bonito flakes. Dashi stock is the base of many soups and noodle dishes in Japan, such as miso, ramen, and soba, and is often available in the Asian or ethnic section of grocery stores or in specialty stores.

Bibimbap

Bibimbap, which means "mixed rice," is a popular Korean dish of warm white rice topped with seasoned vegetables, thinly sliced beef, egg, and *gochujang*. All of these ingredients are served with the rice but not necessarily mixed with it—the choice is yours!

Serves 4

- 4 cups water
- 1 (8-ounce) salmon fillet, lightly seasoned with salt and black pepper
- ½ pound fresh baby spinach
- 3 tablespoons vegetable oil
- 2 large eggs, lightly whisked
- 5 cups warm cooked medium-grain white rice
- ½ medium green bell pepper, seeded and diced
- ½ cup finely chopped kimchi
- 1 tablespoon gochujang
- ¼ cup finely chopped green onions, for garnish
- ½ teaspoon sesame oil, for garnish

1. Add the water to the pot, cover, and set the cooker to Cook. Put the salmon on a plate and place in the steamer basket. When the water boils, place the steamer basket in the rice cooker and steam covered for about 6 minutes or until the salmon cooks through. Remove the salmon from the plate and break the fish into bite-sized pieces.

2. Place the spinach on the steamer plate, insert, and steam covered for 2 minutes until the spinach is tender. Remove the plate, drain any excess liquid, and allow to cool; then cut into long, thin strips (julienne).

3. Clean the pot and wipe it dry. Add the oil, cover, and set to Cook. When the base is warm, add the eggs and cook into an omelet, removing once done. Set aside and cut into thin strips when cool enough to touch.

4. Add the cooked rice, the bell peppers, and kimchi to the pot and mix well. Smooth the top of the rice and then arrange the salmon, eggs, and spinach on top. Cover and set to Warm until ready to serve.

5. Before serving, add the gochujang on top of the rice and garnish with green onions and a drizzle of sesame oil.

Fragrant Coconut Rice

If you can find them, add 4 pandan, or screw pine, leaves to this dish when the coconut milk goes in. These leaves add a sweet-savory scent and can be found in some Asian supermarkets, especially in Hawaii, California, and the Pacific Northwest.

Serves 4

2 cups long-grain white rice
1 cup water
1½ cups canned coconut milk
½ teaspoon salt

1 Rinse the rice with cold water in a strainer or colander. Drain and add to the rice cooker pot.

2 Add the water, coconut milk, and salt; cover and set to Cook. Most automatic rice cookers will switch to Warm when the rice is cooked.

3 After the rice is cooked, do not open the cover immediately. Let it sit to vent off the remaining steam, about 8 minutes, then fluff the rice before serving.

Tomato Rice

Tomato rice is a staple in its native southern India, so there are as almost many recipes for it as there are Indian home cooks. Let this version be your starting point, and once you're comfortable, experiment with ginger, garlic, turmeric, or any other common Indian spice.

Serves 4

2 cups basmati rice
2 tablespoons butter
1 (2-inch) cinnamon stick
½ cup diced tomatoes with juice
2 cups Vegetable Stock (see Chapter 2)
½ teaspoon salt

1 Rinse the rice in cold water, straining through a strainer or colander. Put the rice in a medium bowl and set aside.

2 Add the butter to the pot, cover, and set to Cook. When the base gets warm, add the cinnamon. Cook for 2 minutes.

3 Stir in the tomatoes, stock, salt, and rice. Mix well, cover, and cook until the rice is done.

4 Let rice sit for 8 minutes to vent off some steam, fluff, and serve.

Yellow Rice

If you've ever worked with turmeric, you'll know where the color in this dish comes from. Many a cook has panicked after staining her hands, jeans, and countertops the almost supernatural yellow of turmeric, but don't worry; the turmeric stains will come out. Eventually.

Serves 4

2 cups long-grain white rice
1 tablespoon vegetable oil
1 (2-inch) cinnamon stick
3 cardamom pods
1 star anise pod
1 teaspoon turmeric
1 teaspoon ground cumin
½ teaspoon salt
2½ cups water

1 Rinse the rice in cold water, straining through a strainer or colander. Put the rice in a medium bowl and set aside.

2 Add the oil to the rice cooker pot, cover, and set to Cook. When the base gets warm, add the cinnamon, cardamom, and star anise and cook for about 5 minutes until fragrant.

3 Add the rice, turmeric, cumin, and salt to the pot and mix well. Add the water and cover. Cook until rice is done.

4 Let sit for 8 minutes, fluff, and serve.

Easy Lemon–Buttered Rice

Lemon-buttered rice? If your starting point for rice dishes is any of the cuisines of Asia, this dish may sound odd, but people have been buttering rice for millennia. For those who haven't tried it, this zesty preparation is a revelation.

Serves 4

2 cups long-grain white rice
2 tablespoons butter
2 medium shallots, peeled and thinly sliced
3 cups Chicken or Vegetable Stock (see Chapter 2)
Zest of half a lemon
2 tablespoons lemon juice
¼ teaspoon ground black pepper
¼ teaspoon salt

1 Rinse the rice in cold water, straining through a strainer or colander. Put the rice in a medium bowl and set aside.

2 Add the butter to the rice cooker pot, cover, and set to Cook. When the base of the pot gets warm, add the shallots and cook about 5 minutes until shallots are soft.

3 Add the rice and stir to coat well with butter and shallots. Add the stock to the rice, cover, and cook until the rice is done.

4 Add the lemon zest and drizzle lemon juice into the rice. Mix well by fluffing up the rice. Sprinkle salt and pepper on the rice. Keep the rice cooker at Warm for about 5 minutes before serving.

Chicken Rice

Two essential tips for moist and tender chicken in this Chicken Rice: first, never allow the chicken to come to a boil (simmer at low heat instead), and second, bathe the chicken in an ice-water bath until cold prior to cooking for a moist, tender bird.

Serves 4

- 4 cups cold water, or as needed to immerse the chicken
- 1 (½-inch) piece fresh ginger, sliced
- 3 green onions, cut into finger-length pieces, divided
- 1 pound chicken, preferably legs or a halved chicken
- 2 cups long-grain white rice
- 2 tablespoons vegetable oil
- 3 cloves garlic, peeled and crushed
- 1 teaspoon grated ginger
- 3 cups reserved chicken stock
- ¼ teaspoon salt

1. Add the water to the pot, cover, and set to Cook. When the water boils, add the sliced ginger and half the green onions. Completely immerse the chicken in the pot, cover, and return to a boil.

2. Switch the rice cooker to Warm and allow to simmer covered for 45 minutes.

3. Skim the top of the stock. Switch to Cook and return to a boil. Then switch to Warm again and allow the chicken to simmer covered for 30 minutes.

4. Strain the contents of the rice cooker over a large bowl. Reserve the chicken stock; chop the chicken into bite-sized pieces and set aside.

5. Rinse the rice in cold water, straining through a strainer or colander. Put the rice in a medium bowl and set aside.

6. Add the oil to the rice cooker pot, cover, and set to Cook. When the base of the pot gets warm, add the garlic, grated ginger, remaining green onions, and rinsed rice. Cook for about 2 minutes until fragrant.

7. Slowly stir in 3 cups of the reserved chicken stock and add the salt. Cover and set to Cook until completely done.

8. Let rice sit for 8 minutes to vent off some steam, fluff, and serve with the chopped chicken.

Indian Vegetable Biryani

In Hyderabad, India, where this dish is usually named Dum Biryani, it is slow-cooked. The meat, usually chicken, mutton, or lamb, is layered with the rice and cooked under low flame in a sealed container. Instead of doing that, toss everything into the rice cooker and enjoy the company of your guests!

Serves 4

- 2 cups basmati rice
- 3 tablespoons butter, divided
- 3 medium shallots, peeled and thinly sliced
- ¼ cup cashews
- ¼ cup raisins
- 1 (2-inch) cinnamon stick
- 6 whole cloves
- 6 cardamom pods
- ½ teaspoon turmeric
- ½ cup diced tomatoes with juice
- 2 cups water
- ½ teaspoon salt

1 Rinse the rice in cold water, straining through a strainer or colander. Put the rice in a medium bowl and set aside.

2 Add 2 tablespoons of the butter to the pot, cover, and set to Cook. When the base gets warm, add the shallots. Cook until shallots soften, about 5 minutes. Remove from the pot and set aside, with the rice if you prefer.

3 Add the cashews and the raisins to the pot and cook covered for 2 minutes.

4 Add the remaining butter, the cinnamon, cloves, cardamom, turmeric, and tomatoes. Cook for 3 more minutes.

5 Stir in the rice and shallots, add the water and salt, and cook covered until the rice is done.

6 Let rice sit for 8 minutes to vent off some steam, fluff, and serve.

Clay-Pot Rice

In traditional clay-pot cooking, the food inside an unglazed clay pot is cooked over a charcoal fire, giving the finished dish a distinctive aromatic flavor. This recipe adapts all of that for your rice cooker.

Serves 3

2 tablespoons oyster sauce
1 tablespoon soy sauce
½ teaspoon sesame oil
½ teaspoon ground white pepper
¼ teaspoon brown sugar
1 tablespoon Chinese cooking wine
½ teaspoon corn flour
½ pound chicken (thighs, breasts, or drumsticks), chopped into bite-sized pieces
2 cups long-grain white rice
3 tablespoons vegetable oil
1 teaspoon grated ginger
6 fresh shiitake mushroom caps, thinly sliced
3 cups water
2 green onions, finely chopped

1 In a medium bowl, add the chicken, oyster sauce, soy sauce, sesame oil, pepper, brown sugar, Chinese cooking wine, and corn flour; add the chicken and stir to combine. Let the chicken marinate in the refrigerator for 1–2 hours.

2 Rinse the rice in cold water, straining through a strainer or colander. Put the rice in a medium bowl and set aside.

3 Add the vegetable oil to the rice cooker, cover, and set to Cook. When the base gets warm, add the ginger, mushrooms, and the chicken along with the marinade. Cook for 5 minutes, covered and stirring occasionally. Transfer all of the chicken and half of the sauce to a separate bowl and set aside.

4 Set to Warm, add the rice and the water, and mix well with the sauce in the cooker pot. Cover and set to Cook. Shortly before the rice is cooked, return the chicken and the reserved half of the sauce to the rice cooker. Cook until done.

5 Switch to Warm for 15 minutes before serving. Garnish with green onions.

Asian "Risotto"

In some parts of Asia, such as Hong Kong, Singapore, and Malaysia, rice is served soaked in thick gravy and is somewhat similar to risotto. Here's a tip: using a frozen seafood mix of items such as shrimp, baby scallops, and calamari will greatly reduce prep and shopping time.

Serves 4

2 tablespoons vegetable oil

12 medium shrimp, peeled, deveined, and diced

½ cup baby scallops

3 cloves garlic, peeled and finely minced

1 teaspoon grated ginger

4 fresh shiitake mushrooms caps, diced

2 cups broccoli florets, blanched

1 tablespoon oyster sauce

2 cups hot water

¼ teaspoon salt

¼ teaspoon ground white pepper

2 large eggs, lightly whisked

4 cups cooked Long-Grain White Rice (see Chapter 2)

1 Add the oil to the pot, cover, and set to Cook. When the base gets warm, add the shrimp, baby scallops, garlic, and ginger. Cook until shrimp turn pink, about 6 minutes. Remove seafood and half the cooking liquid and set aside.

2 Add the mushrooms, broccoli, oyster sauce, and water and stir well. Cover and bring to a simmer. Return the seafood to the pot and add the salt and pepper. Cover and cook, stirring occasionally, until pot returns to a boil and the liquid begins to reduce.

3 Switch the rice cooker to Warm and slowly add the whisked eggs. Swirl the eggs gently in one direction using a chopstick. The warmth of the cooked ingredients will set the egg to a runny and creamy texture.

4 Pour the seafood and egg gravy on top of the cooked rice and serve immediately.

Pumpkin Rice

What could be a more American dish than this Pumpkin Rice? Sublime as a side dish at your favorite late-November feast and tasty any time of year, this rice preparation is elevated to the next level by the earthy, savory flavor of the shiitake mushrooms.

Serves 4

- 2 cups long-grain white rice
- 2 tablespoons vegetable oil
- ½ pound lean pork, sliced less than ¼-inch thick
- 6 fresh shiitake mushroom caps, diced
- 2 cloves garlic, peeled and finely minced
- 3 medium shallots, peeled and thinly sliced
- 1 cup diced fresh pumpkin
- ¼ teaspoon salt
- ¼ teaspoon ground white pepper
- 3 cups water

1 Rinse the rice in cold water, straining through a strainer or colander. Put the rice in a medium bowl and set aside.

2 Add the oil to the cooker pot, cover, and set to Cook. When the base warms, add the pork, mushrooms, garlic, and shallots and cook for 5 minutes until the surface of the pork browns. Dish out and set aside.

3 Add the pumpkin and the salt to whatever oil remains in the pot and cook about 3 minutes. Add the pepper and the rinsed rice to the pot along with the water.

4 Return the pork mixture to the pot and mix well. Cover and cook until rice is done.

5 Before serving, let the rice sit at Warm about 8 minutes to release some of the remaining steam.

Savory Cabbage Rice

The "savory" in this dish doesn't refer to the cabbage itself; when simmered and cooked until soft and tender, round cabbage actually becomes sweeter. It's this naturally sweet quality that lends such a perfect balance to the savory goodness of the lean cuts of pork.

Serves 4

1 teaspoon oyster sauce

1 teaspoon soy sauce

½ cup hot water

2 cups long-grain white rice

2 tablespoons vegetable oil

½ pound lean pork, thinly sliced less than ¼-inch thick

6 fresh shiitake mushrooms caps, diced

2 cloves garlic, peeled and finely minced

3 medium shallots, peeled and thinly sliced

½ pound round cabbage, thinly sliced

¼ teaspoon ground white pepper

3 cups water

1 Mix oyster sauce, soy sauce, and hot water in a small bowl. Set aside.

2 Rinse the rice in cold water, straining through a strainer or colander. Put the rice in a medium bowl and set aside.

3 Add the oil to the rice cooker, cover, and set to Cook. When the base of the pot gets warm, add the pork, mushrooms, garlic, and shallots and cook for 5 minutes until the pork is browned. Transfer the pork mixture to a medium bowl using a slotted spoon and set aside.

4 Add the cabbage to any remaining oil in the pot and cook for about 3 minutes until tender. Add the pepper and the sauce mixture to the pot, mix well, and cook for about 1 minute. Dish out and set aside.

5 Add the rice and 3 cups water to the pot and cook. When the rice is almost done, return the pork and cabbage mixture to the pot. Cook until done.

6 Set cooker to Warm and let sit covered 15 minutes before serving.

Savory Taro Rice

Taro is one Asia-Pacific staple that has yet to become a mainstream food in the US. Here and there, some parents have taken to poi, the traditional Hawaiian taro preparation, as a fiber- and vitamin-packed baby food. Taro is otherwise found largely in Asian groceries, so look for it there.

Serves 4

2 cups long-grain white rice

2 tablespoons vegetable oil

½ pound lean pork, cut into ½-inch cubes

4 fresh shiitake mushrooms caps, diced

2 cloves garlic, peeled and finely minced

3 medium shallots, peeled and thinly sliced

2 cups diced taro, cut into ½-inch cubes

½ teaspoon ground white pepper

¼ teaspoon salt

3 cups water

1 teaspoon oyster sauce

1 teaspoon soy sauce

1 green onion, thinly sliced, for garnish

1 Rinse the rice in cold water, straining through a strainer or colander. Put the rice in a medium bowl and set aside.

2 Add the oil to the rice cooker, cover, and set to Cook. When the base of the pot gets warm, add the pork, mushrooms, garlic, and shallots and cook, stirring occasionally, about 3 minutes until pork is browned on the surface. Dish out and set aside.

3 Add the taro, the pepper, and the salt and cook for 3 minutes.

4 Add the rice, water, oyster sauce, and soy sauce and mix well.

5 Return the pork mixture to the pot, stirring vigorously. Cover and cook until rice is done.

6 Let the steam vent about 8 minutes before serving. Fluff and serve garnished with the green onion.

Beef Fried Rice

This fried rice, as Tex-Mex as it is Asian, is hearty and savory like many other "dirty rice" dishes found in the US. Remember that ground beef cooks quickly and easily, so be sure not to overdo it.

Serves 2

3 tablespoons vegetable oil

3 medium shallots, peeled and thinly sliced

½ pound ground beef

¼ cup warm water

4 cups warm cooked medium-grain white rice

¼ teaspoon salt

¼ teaspoon ground black pepper

1 green onion, finely chopped, for garnish

1 Add the oil to the rice cooker, cover, and set to Cook. When the base warms, add the shallots and cook for about 8 minutes until slightly soft and caramelized.

2 Add the ground beef and cook for 10 minutes, covered and stirring occasionally until browned.

3 Stir in the water, cover the rice cooker, and cook for 2 minutes. Switch to Warm and simmer for 10 minutes until completely cooked. Add the cooked rice and mix well with the beef and shallots. Add the salt and pepper.

4 Keep the rice cooker at Warm for 15 minutes before serving. Garnish with the green onions.

Egg and Shrimp Fried Rice

When cooking fried rice over the stovetop, many cooks become frustrated by the rice sticking to the pan and/or clumping up. You and your rice cooker don't have to worry—the material your rice cooker is made of and the cooking temperature help prevent both!

Serves 2

- 3 tablespoons oil, divided
- 2 cloves garlic, peeled and finely minced
- ½ cup frozen peas, thawed
- 2 large eggs, lightly whisked
- 12 medium shrimp, peeled, deveined, and diced
- 4 cups warm cooked medium-grain white rice
- 1 teaspoon soy sauce
- ¼ teaspoon salt
- ¼ teaspoon ground black pepper
- 1 green onion, finely chopped, for garnish
- 1 fresh red chili pepper, seeded and thinly sliced, for garnish

1 Add 1½ tablespoons of the oil to the rice cooker, cover, and set to Cook. When the base of the pot gets warm, add the garlic and peas and sauté for about 5 minutes until the peas are tender. Remove from pot and set aside.

2 Add the remaining 1½ tablespoons of oil to the rice cooker pot. Add the eggs and gently scramble them in the pot.

3 Add the shrimp and cook for about 8 minutes until shrimp and egg are cooked. Add the cooked rice, soy sauce, and pea mixture to the pot and mix well.

4 Keep the rice cooker at Warm for about 15 minutes before serving. Sprinkle with salt and black pepper and garnish with green onion and red chili.

Shrimp Pilaf

By definition, "pilaf" means rice cooked in seasoned broth with poultry or seafood and sometimes tomatoes. In the United States, pilaf is usually served as a side dish accompanying a main course such as grilled fish. Indian Vegetable Biryani (see recipe in this chapter) is also considered a kind of pilaf.

Serves 4

2 cups basmati rice

2 tablespoons butter, divided

6 medium shallots, peeled and thinly sliced

1½ cups diced tomatoes, with juice

½ teaspoon chili powder

1 teaspoon grated ginger

½ teaspoon garam masala

½ teaspoon salt

½ cup water

2 pounds medium shrimp, peeled and deveined

1 (2-inch) cinnamon stick

4 cardamom pods

6 whole cloves

2½ cups Shrimp Stock (see Chapter 2)

½ cup finely chopped fresh cilantro, for garnish

1   Rinse the rice in cold water, straining through a strainer or colander. Put the rice in a medium bowl and set aside.

2   Add 1 tablespoon of the butter to the rice cooker pot, cover, and set to Cook. When the base of the cooker pot gets warm, add the shallots and cook until soft, about 3 minutes.

3   Add the tomatoes and chili powder and cook for about 2 minutes. Add the ginger, garam masala, salt, and water. Mix well. Stir in the shrimp and cook for about 8 minutes, covered and stirring occasionally, until the shrimp turn pink and the liquid slightly reduces. Dish out the shrimp mixture and set aside.

4   Add the remaining 1 tablespoon of butter to the rice cooker pot. When the base of the cooker pot gets warm, add the cinnamon, cardamom, and cloves and cook until fragrant.

5   Add the rice and Shrimp Stock to the pot and mix well with the spices. Cover the rice cooker, switch to Cook, and cook until done.

6   Let cooked rice sit for 8 minutes to vent off the remaining steam. Fluff the rice and gently slide the shrimp mixture back over the top of the rice before serving. Garnish with cilantro.

Seafood Fried Rice

Oyster sauce appears everywhere in Asian cooking. If you prefer not to use the real thing, whether because you're avoiding shellfish or meat in general, look for a mushroom sauce. Many grocers now carry them, and they're about as close a substitute as you're likely to find.

Serves 2

3 tablespoons vegetable oil

12 medium shrimp, peeled, deveined, and tails left on

½ cup baby scallops

2 cloves garlic, peeled and finely minced

3 medium shallots, peeled and thinly sliced

1 cup diced string beans

½ cup frozen corn, thawed

½ cup frozen green peas, thawed

1 teaspoon oyster sauce

1 tablespoon warm water

3 cups warm cooked medium-grain white rice

1 fresh red chili pepper, thinly sliced, for garnish

1 Add the oil to the rice cooker, cover, and set to Cook. When the base of the pot gets warm, add the shrimp, baby scallops, garlic, and shallots and cook about 8 minutes until shrimp and scallops are cooked (the shrimp should be pink and the scallops white). Dish out seafood and set aside.

2 Add the beans, corn, and peas to the rice cooker and cook for about 5 minutes until vegetables are just tender.

3 Return the seafood to the pot, add the oyster sauce and warm water, and mix well.

4 Add the cooked rice to the rice cooker and mix well with seafood and vegetables. Cover rice cooker.

5 Switch rice cooker to Warm and let sit 15 minutes before serving. Garnish with red chili.

Spicy Rice with Peppers and Pine Nuts

You can try a different variety of nuts in this recipe, but remember to chop finely, especially any nuts that are larger. This helps give the rice a balanced bite and texture and assures you'll have a consistent bite in every spoonful.

Serves 4

- 2 cups long-grain white rice
- 3 cups Chicken Stock (see Chapter 2), or as needed
- ½ teaspoon turmeric
- 1 star anise pod
- 4 cardamom pods
- 4 whole cloves
- ½ cup diced green bell peppers
- ½ cup diced red bell peppers
- ½ cup pine nuts
- ¼ teaspoon salt
- ¼ teaspoon ground black pepper

1 Rinse the rice in cold water, straining through a strainer or colander.

2 Add the rice to the rice cooker pot along with enough Chicken Stock to cover the rice by about ½ inch. Add the turmeric, star anise, cardamom, and cloves and mix well. Cover, set to Cook, and cook until the rice is done.

3 When the rice is cooked, top with the bell peppers and the pine nuts.

4 Set the rice cooker to Warm for about 15 minutes, then add the salt and black pepper and fluff up the rice to serve.

Forms of Cardamom

Cardamom comes in several forms: the pod, which is the preferred form and retains aroma and flavor for a long period; the seed, which is generally crushed or ground prior to use; and ground cardamom, which is usually used because it's the most convenient but compromises slightly on freshness and full flavor.

Beef and Rice Soup

Beef and rice strike a surprisingly sublime note when simmered with soy sauce and cooking wine, as in this recipe. Although this Beef and Rice Soup is a perfect dish to serve in the winter, it's not as heavy as you may imagine and bursts with flavor in any season.

Serves 4

- 2 tablespoons butter
- 3 medium shallots, peeled and thinly sliced
- 2 cloves garlic, peeled and finely minced
- ½ pound ground beef
- 1 teaspoon soy sauce
- ½ teaspoon ground white pepper
- 1 teaspoon Chinese cooking wine
- 8 cups water
- 3 cups warm cooked medium-grain white rice, divided among 4 serving bowls
- 3 green onions, thinly sliced, for garnish

1 Add the butter to the rice cooker, cover, and set to Cook. When the base of the pot gets warm, add the shallots and cook for about 5 minutes until shallots are soft.

2 Add the garlic and continue to cook for about 1 minute. Add the ground beef, soy sauce, and pepper. Cook for 8 minutes, covered and stirring frequently.

3 Add the Chinese cooking wine and cook for 1 minute. Add the water and cover. When the mixture boils, switch to Warm and simmer for about 15 minutes or until cooked through.

4 Ladle the soup over cooked rice in serving bowls. Garnish with green onions.

Fish Kedgeree

Traditionally, kedgeree is a dish of flaked fish, cooked rice, hard-boiled eggs, and butter. Make it flexible, your way, by using leftover cooked fish (preferably grilled), fresh fish cooked on the same day, or canned fish.

Serves 4

- 4 cups water
- ½ pound salmon
- 2 tablespoons butter
- 3 medium shallots, peeled and thinly sliced
- 2 cloves garlic, peeled and finely minced
- 5 cups warm cooked long-grain white rice
- 2 hard-boiled eggs, peeled and chopped
- 2 green onions, finely chopped
- ¼ cup finely chopped fresh cilantro
- ¼ teaspoon ground black pepper
- ¼ teaspoon salt

1. Add the water to the pot, cover, and set the cooker to Cook. While the water is coming to a boil, place the salmon on a plate and fit into the steamer basket. When the water boils, place the basket in the rice cooker, cover, and steam for 8 minutes or until the salmon turns a light pink-orange. Break the salmon into bite-sized flakes and set aside.

2. Clean out the rice cooker and wipe dry. Add the butter, cover, and set to Cook. When the bottom gets warm, add the shallots and cook about 3 minutes until soft.

3. Add the garlic and continue to cook for about 1 minute. Add the cooked rice and flaked salmon and mix well to incorporate all the flavors.

4. Top with hard-boiled eggs, green onions, cilantro, pepper, and salt. Switch rice cooker to Warm and allow it to sit for 5–10 minutes before serving.

Congee and Porridge Dishes

Silky and comforting, *congee* is a Chinese word meaning "wet rice." In the West it's known as rice porridge; in Korea and elsewhere it's called jook. Congee is traditionally served in Asia for breakfast, and though it's a wonderful way to start the day, congee is also consumed as a side dish or main dish for lunch and dinner depending on the ingredients added. It is prepared with a higher ratio of water to rice than traditional rice cooking. This allows the starch from the rice to create a lovely and creamy bowl of comfort food. From Fish Congee and Pumpkin Porridge to Goji Berry Congee and Pork Congee, enjoy a full meal with this chapter's well-rounded bowls of porridge.

Fish Congee

There are two common types of fish congee in Asia. As in this recipe, the fish is cooked together with the rice porridge, and the finished dish has a thick, porridge-like consistency. The other is a fish soup ladled over fish slices and rice, similar to Halibut-Asparagus Soup with Pancetta (see Chapter 4).

Serves 2

1 cup long-grain white rice

2 (8-ounce) fish fillets (snapper, cod, or sea bass if possible), cut into ¼-inch-thick slices

¼ teaspoon salt

¼ teaspoon ground white pepper

1 teaspoon sesame oil, divided

1 teaspoon Chinese cooking wine

5 cups water (use less water for thicker consistency)

1 (1-inch) piece fresh ginger, thinly sliced

¼ cup finely chopped green onions, for garnish

¼ cup fried ginger strips, for garnish

1 Rinse the rice in cold water, straining through a strainer or colander. Set aside.

2 In a medium bowl, add the fish slices, salt, pepper, ½ teaspoon sesame oil, and Chinese cooking wine and stir to combine. Cover and place in the refrigerator to marinate.

3 Add the rice and the water to the rice cooker, cover, and set to Cook. When it comes to a boil, uncover and add the fresh ginger slices.

4 Stir and continue to cook for 40 minutes, partially covered and stirring occasionally.

5 Add the marinated fish slices to the congee, partially cover the pot, and return to a boil. The fish is done when it turns opaque, about 5 minutes.

6 Dish out congee into serving bowls and drizzle with remaining sesame oil. Garnish with green onions and fried ginger strips before serving.

Seafood Congee

Many modern dishes don't go back as far as we may like to think, but congee is not among them. A reference appears in a fourth-century text attributing congee to the Yellow Emperor, a mythic ancient king whose reign is said to have ended nearly five millennia ago.

Serves 2

1 cup long-grain white rice

4 cups water

1 (1-inch) piece fresh ginger, thinly sliced

½ cup medium shrimp, peeled, deveined, and diced

½ cup fresh baby scallops

1 (8-ounce) cod fillet, thinly sliced

½ teaspoon ground white pepper

2 green onions, finely chopped, for garnish

1. Rinse the rice in cold water, straining through a strainer or colander.

2. Add the rice and the water to the rice cooker pot, cover, and set to Cook. When it comes to a boil and bubbles to the top of the pot, add the ginger and stir well. Simmer for 45 minutes, partially covered and stirring occasionally, until the rice turns into a soft pulp.

3. Stir in shrimp, scallops, fish slices, and pepper. Partially cover rice cooker and simmer for 20 minutes until seafood cooks through. Garnish with green onions.

Pork Congee

Chinese chefs often mix rice grains in congee, which helps create a smooth texture. Try stirring the rice at intervals during cooking and simmering. This will break up the whole grains and makes for a smooth, creamy porridge.

Serves 2

- 2 tablespoons vegetable oil
- ½ pound lean pork strips, about ¼-inch thick
- 4 fresh shiitake mushroom caps, thinly sliced
- ½ teaspoon soy sauce
- 2 cloves garlic, peeled and thinly sliced
- ¼ teaspoon salt
- ¼ teaspoon ground black pepper
- 1 cup long-grain white rice
- 4 cups water (use a bit less for a thicker consistency)
- ½ teaspoon ground white pepper
- 2 green onions, finely chopped, for garnish

1. Add the oil to the rice cooker, cover, and set to Cook. When the base of the pot gets warm, add the pork, mushrooms, soy sauce, garlic, salt, and black pepper. Cook for 8 minutes until fragrant, covering the rice cooker intermittently. Dish out half of the pork mixture and set aside in a bowl.

2. Rinse the rice in cold water, straining through a strainer or colander.

3. Add the rice to the remaining pork mixture, stirring well. Slowly pour in the water, cover the rice cooker, and allow the mixture to come to a boil. When the liquid begins to bubble over, lift the cover and add the reserved pork mixture and stir gently.

4. Simmer partially covered and stirring occasionally about 45 minutes or until rice turns soft and pulpy. Season with the white pepper and garnish with the green onions before serving.

Chicken Congee

The flavor of fresh, young ginger—you'll find it by its scent and its slightly less knotted appearance in the produce aisle—is substantially more powerful than that of older cuts and less bitter than the dried and ground herb.

Serves 4

1 cup long-grain white rice

5 cups Chicken Stock (see Chapter 2)

½ pound boneless chicken thighs and breasts, cut into thin strips

1 (½-inch) piece fresh ginger, finely shredded

¼ teaspoon salt

¼ teaspoon ground white pepper

¼ teaspoon sesame oil, for drizzling

1 green onion, finely chopped, for garnish

1 Rinse the rice in cold water, straining through a strainer or colander.

2 Add the rice and stock to the pot, cover, and set to Cook. When the pot begins to bubble over, adjust the lid so that the pot is partially covered. Simmer about 40 minutes, stirring occasionally, until the rice is soft and pulpy.

3 Stir in the chicken, ginger, salt, and pepper. Simmer, still set to Cook and partially covered, another 15 minutes or until chicken is cooked through.

4 Continue cooking, adding water as needed, until your desired consistency is reached. Drizzle with sesame oil, garnish with the green onions, and serve.

Sweet Potato Porridge

Adding sweet potatoes to rice porridge seems to have originated during World War II, when rice was expensive and sweet potatoes were abundant. The sweet potatoes provide a consistency and flavor that makes this dish especially distinctive.

Serves 4

1 cup long-grain white rice
4 cups water (use a bit less for a thicker consistency)
1 medium sweet potato, peeled and cut into 1-inch chunks
¼ teaspoon salt

1. Rinse the rice in cold water, straining through a strainer or colander.

2. Add the rice and the water to the rice cooker, cover, and set to Cook. When the pot begins to bubble over, uncover and add the sweet potatoes and salt. Cook about 40 minutes partially covered and stirring occasionally.

Tuna and Corn Congee

Have you noticed some changes in the canned fish aisle? Many markets now carry line-caught tuna, which is a more expensive but much more ecologically sound product, as it nearly eliminates bycatch, the wasteful and indiscriminate loss of unmarketable sea life that comes with net fishing for tuna.

Serves 3

1 cup long-grain white rice
5 cups water (use less water for thicker consistency)
1 cup flaked canned tuna
1 cup canned corn kernels, drained
¼ teaspoon ground white pepper

1. Rinse the rice in cold water, straining through a strainer or colander.

2. Add the rice and water to the rice cooker, cover, and set to Cook. When the liquid starts to bubble over, stir the congee, partially recover, and cook about 40 minutes. Stir occasionally.

3. Add the tuna, corn, and pepper and continue cooking, stirring occasionally, for 15–20 minutes.

4. Continue cooking, adding water as needed, until your desired consistency is reached.

Pumpkin Porridge

Pumpkin brings a mild sweetness to porridge, and it complements the savory flavor of the pork. These elements aren't often combined in traditional American cooking, but give this Pumpkin Porridge a try and you'll immediately wonder, why not!

Serves 3

- 2 tablespoons vegetable oil
- 1 cup diced pumpkin
- ½ pound ground pork
- 2 fresh shiitake mushroom caps, finely diced
- ½ teaspoon soy sauce
- 2 cloves garlic, peeled and finely minced
- ¼ teaspoon salt
- ¼ teaspoon ground black pepper
- 1 cup long-grain white rice
- 4 cups water (use a bit less for a thicker consistency)
- ½ teaspoon ground white pepper
- 2 green onions, finely chopped, for garnish

1 Add the oil to the pot, cover, and set to Cook. When the base warms, add the pumpkin, pork, mushrooms, soy sauce, garlic, salt, and black pepper. Cook covered and stirring occasionally until fragrant, about 7 minutes.

2 Dish half the mixture into a medium bowl and set aside. Rinse the rice in cold water, straining through a strainer or colander. Add the rinsed rice to the rice cooker pot, stirring to mix well.

3 Slowly add the water, cover, and bring to a boil. When the mixture begins to bubble over, add the reserved pork mixture; continue to cook stirring frequently and partially covered about 40 minutes until the rice turns to a soft pulp.

4 Season with the white pepper and garnish with the green onions before serving.

Stir It Smooth

In many Chinese restaurants, congee is served so smooth that you can't even make out individual grains. There's a trick to this almost otherworldly smoothness, and it's elaborate and involves using several different grains of rice, but if you stir the rice mixture steadily, slowly, and as often as possible while cooking, you just might come close.

Goji Berry Congee

Goji berry has been touted as a superfood in recent years thanks to its bevy of antioxidants, nutrients, and fiber. In traditional Chinese medicine, goji berry is also a natural supplement known to relieve eye strain.

Serves 3

1 cup long-grain white rice
4 cups water (use a bit less for a thicker consistency)
½ cup dried goji berries, soaked in warm water

1 Rinse the rice in cold water, straining through a strainer or colander.

2 Add the rice and water to the rice cooker pot, cover, and set to Cook. When the pot begins to bubble over, uncover and stir. Cook partially covered and stirring occasionally, about 40 minutes, until rice reaches a soft pulp.

3 Stir in goji berries about 5 minutes before serving, but not before: overcooked berries will take on a bitter flavor that diminishes the dish.

Corn, Carrot, and Pea Congee

It almost goes without saying that fresh vegetables are preferable to frozen ones, but there are exceptions. This is one—when added while still frozen, the vegetables hold up much better to the cooking process.

Serves 2

1 cup long-grain white rice

4 cups Chicken Stock (see Chapter 2)

2 cups frozen mixed vegetables (corn, carrots, and peas)

½ teaspoon salt

¼ teaspoon ground white pepper

2 green onions, finely chopped, for garnish

1 Rinse the rice in cold water, straining through a strainer or colander.

2 Add the rice and stock to the rice cooker pot, cover, and set to Cook. When the pot begins to bubble over, partially uncover and continue to simmer stirring occasionally until rice takes on the consistency of oatmeal, about 40 minutes.

3 Add the vegetables, salt, and pepper and continue cooking for 15–20 minutes.

4 Garnish with the green onions and serve.

Taro and Spinach Congee

Congee is a common Chinese home remedy for the symptoms of colds and flu. It is believed that the cooking liquid in which the congee is simmered can boost both the immune system and energy level. The liquid also prevents the dehydration that can occur with a cold or the flu.

Serves 2

2 tablespoons vegetable oil

½ pound lean pork strips, about ¼-inch thick

1 cup peeled and cubed taro

½ teaspoon soy sauce

¼ teaspoon salt

¼ teaspoon ground black pepper

1 cup long-grain white rice

4 cups water (use less water for thicker consistency)

3 tightly packed cups fresh baby spinach

1 Add the oil to the pot, cover, and set to Cook. When the base of the pot is warm, add the pork, taro cubes, soy sauce, salt, and pepper. Cook until fragrant, about 6 minutes. Dish out the pork and taro mixture and set aside in a medium bowl.

2 Rinse the rice in cold water, straining through a strainer or colander.

3 Add the rice and water to the rice cooker and cover. When the pot begins to bubble over, add the pork and taro mixture, stirring well. Cook partially covered and stirring occasionally for about 30 minutes.

4 About 5 minutes before serving, stir in the spinach.

Pasta Fusion Main Dishes

We know rice can be cooked flawlessly in the rice cooker, so doesn't it just make sense that pasta can be just as amazing? It generally requires no draining. The recipes in this chapter celebrate the combination of different meats, vegetables, and spices to create a medley of flavors and meals. From Beef and Shiitake Pasta and Pasta Arrabiata to Spicy Italian Sausage Pasta and Easy Shrimp and Celery Pasta Salad, these recipes will have your taste buds dancing while the pasta gives you that carb comfort that is sometimes needed after a grueling day.

Fish Pasta

Don't worry if you can't find or don't like snapper; this light, tasty dish isn't particular and will work with just about any boneless fillet. If you're cooking something like ahi or swordfish, you'll want to add a bit of cooking time accordingly.

Serves 2

- 1 (6-ounce) snapper fillet, cut into ¼-inch-thick slices
- ½ teaspoon salt, divided
- ½ teaspoon ground black pepper, divided
- 3 tablespoons extra-virgin olive oil
- 1 large onion, peeled and thinly sliced
- 3 cloves garlic, peeled and finely minced
- 1 (14½-ounce) can diced tomatoes, with juice
- ½ cup Shrimp Stock (see Chapter 2)
- ½ pound fusilli or other pasta, cooked
- ½ teaspoon dried oregano
- ½ teaspoon dried basil

1 Sprinkle the fish with ¼ teaspoon salt and ¼ teaspoon pepper. Set aside.

2 Add the oil to the rice cooker, cover, and set to Cook. When the base of the pot gets warm, add the fish slices, cover, and cook for about 3 minutes per side until the fish cooks through. Remove from pot and set aside.

3 Using the remaining oil in the pot, add the onions and cook until soft, translucent, and slightly caramelized, about 8 minutes.

4 Add the garlic and cook 2 minutes more.

5 Stir in the tomatoes and stock and cover. When the sauce starts to boil, uncover and continue to simmer until sauce reduces slightly, about 5 minutes. Add remaining ¼ teaspoon salt and pepper.

6 Switch rice cooker to Warm. Add the cooked pasta and mix with sauce. Add the oregano and basil and mix well. Divide pasta into serving bowls, top with fish slices, and serve.

Beef and Shiitake Pasta

Most mushrooms you find at the grocery store—white, cremini, brown, even portobello—are different varietals and maturities of the same single species. Shiitake are distinct. Native to Asia, they carry a bigger, bolder flavor and are often paired with or even substituted for meat.

Serves 2

- 2 tablespoons extra-virgin olive oil
- 1 medium onion, peeled and thinly sliced
- ½ tablespoon butter
- 3 cloves garlic, peeled and finely minced
- ½ pound ground beef
- 6 fresh shiitake mushroom caps, thinly sliced
- 1 (14½-ounce) can diced tomatoes, with juice
- 1 cup Vegetable Stock (see Chapter 2)
- ¼ teaspoon salt
- ¼ teaspoon ground black pepper
- ½ pound fusilli, cooked
- ½ teaspoon dried basil, for garnish

1 Add the oil to the rice cooker, cover, and set to Cook. When the base of the pot gets warm, add the onions and cook until slightly soft, about 4 minutes. Add the butter and garlic and cook for about 2 more minutes. Add the ground beef and mix well with the other ingredients. Cook for about 4 minutes until beef turns brown on the surface. Remove from pot and set aside.

2 Add the mushrooms, tomatoes, and stock to the pot. Mix well and cover the rice cooker. When the sauce mixture starts to boil, return the reserved beef to the rice cooker and allow mixture to come to a slight simmer. Uncover and simmer about 10 minutes until sauce reduces slightly and beef cooks through.

3 Add the salt and pepper. Switch rice cooker to Warm. Add the cooked pasta and mix thoroughly with the sauce. Garnish with basil and serve.

Chicken and Shrimp Pasta

For crisper, greener broccoli, try shocking it. Boil the florets for 30 seconds, then plunge them into an ice-water bath. This "shocking" process stops cooking the broccoli and helps to preserve its nice green color.

Serves 2

- 2 tablespoons vegetable oil
- 3 cloves garlic, peeled and finely minced
- ¼ pound boneless chicken (thigh and breast), chopped into bite-sized pieces
- 8–10 medium shrimp, peeled, deveined, and tails left on
- 1 teaspoon oyster sauce
- 1 cup Chicken Stock (see Chapter 2)
- ¼ teaspoon salt
- ¼ teaspoon ground white pepper
- ½ pound shell pasta, cooked
- 1 cup broccoli florets
- 1 fresh red chili pepper, seeded and thinly sliced, for garnish

1 Add the oil to the rice cooker, cover, and set to Cook. When the base of the pot gets warm, add the garlic and cook for 1 minute.

2 Add the chicken and cook for 5 minutes, covered and stirring frequently, until the chicken is almost cooked through. Add the shrimp and cook for 4 more minutes until the shrimp turn pink and cook through. The chicken should finish cooking as well.

3 Add the oyster sauce and stock, cover, and bring to a boil. Switch the rice cooker to Warm and continue to simmer for about 8 minutes until sauce slightly reduces.

4 Add the salt and white pepper, cooked pasta, and broccoli and mix well. When the liquid gets mostly absorbed into the pasta, dish out and serve garnished with the sliced red chili.

Macaroni and Chicken

Macaroni is also known as epoundow pasta and is one of the world's most popular noodles. Too many of us know it these days only through mac-and-cheese boxes, but it's also perfect for soups, salads, and casseroles.

Serves 2

6 cups water, or enough to immerse the chicken

4 celery stalks, cut into bite-sized pieces

1 medium carrot, peeled and cut into bite-sized pieces

½ pound chicken thighs and breasts

½ pound macaroni, cooked

1 green onion, finely chopped

¼ teaspoon salt

¼ teaspoon ground white pepper

1 Add the water to the pot, cover, and set to Cook. When the water boils, add the celery and carrots and completely immerse the chicken in the water. Cover and return to a boil.

2 Switch the rice cooker to Warm and simmer for about 45 minutes or until the chicken cooks through.

3 Dish out the chicken and thinly shred it. Set aside.

4 Divide the macaroni among the serving bowls, top with shredded chicken, and ladle soup, celery, and carrots over the macaroni.

5 Top with green onions, salt, and white pepper.

Make Sure You're Ready to Serve

When not serving this dish immediately, remove the celery and carrots once they are cooked. If they are kept warm in the rice cooker for too long, they turn limp and discolored. When ready to serve, spoon the chicken, celery, and carrots on top of the macaroni in the serving bowls and ladle warm soup over the macaroni.

Tomato and Shrimp Pasta

Will you decide to dice the tomatoes yourself or go with the canned? If so, what kind of tomatoes will you use? Cherry and grape tomatoes don't hold up to dicing very well, but in general, the smaller the tomato, the more tart the taste.

Serves 2

2 tablespoons extra-virgin olive oil

3 medium shallots, peeled and thinly sliced

12 medium shrimp, peeled, deveined, and diced

1 (14½-ounce) can diced tomatoes, with juice

¼ teaspoon salt

¼ teaspoon ground black pepper

½ pound fusilli, cooked

¼ teaspoon dried oregano, for garnish

1 Add the oil to the pot, cover, and set to Cook. When the base of the pot gets warm, add the shallots and cook until slightly soft, about 5 minutes.

2 Add the shrimp and cook for 4 minutes or until shrimp turn pink. Add the tomatoes, mix well, cover the rice cooker, and allow to come to a slight simmer.

3 Uncover and add the salt and pepper and cook until sauce reduces slightly.

4 Add the cooked pasta and mix well. Garnish with oregano before serving.

Creamy Mushroom Pasta

There are so many pasta shapes—shell, tubular, strand—that it's sometimes tempting to grab whatever's handy. Try not to. Different pasta shapes carry sauces in different ways and make a difference in the experience of the dish. Fusilli's spiral shape is perfect for this recipe.

Serves 2

- 2 tablespoons extra-virgin olive oil
- ½ tablespoon butter
- 3 medium shallots, peeled and thinly sliced
- 2 cups thinly sliced white or brown mushrooms
- ¼ teaspoon salt
- ¼ teaspoon ground black pepper
- 1 cup whole milk
- ½ pound fusilli, cooked
- ¼ cup grated Cheddar cheese
- ¼ cup grated Parmesan cheese

1. Add the oil and butter to the rice cooker, cover, and set to Cook. When the base of the pot gets warm, add the shallots and cook until shallots are slightly soft, about 5 minutes.

2. Add the mushrooms and cook, covered, stirring frequently for 8 minutes or until mushrooms are tender.

3. Add the salt and pepper. Slowly stir the milk into the pot. Cover and bring to a slight simmer. When simmering, stir the milk sauce constantly for 5 minutes or until it reduces slightly.

4. Add the cooked pasta to the sauce and stir until the sauce reduces further.

5. Top with the cheeses. Serve immediately.

Want a Thicker Sauce?

For a thicker sauce, use 1 cup heavy cream instead of milk, or ½ cup heavy cream and ½ cup whole milk.

Pasta Arrabbiata

Arrabbiata is a sauce traditionally made from garlic, tomatoes, basil, and red chili cooked in olive oil. It's usually served with pasta and chopped fresh parsley, and if you make this without the shrimp, it's a great sauce to make in advance and freeze for use in a pinch.

Serves 2

1 tablespoon butter

12 medium shrimp, peeled and deveined

2 cups marinara sauce

4 whole red dried chili peppers

½ pound fusilli, cooked

½ teaspoon dried oregano, for garnish

1 Add the butter to the rice cooker pot, cover, and set to Cook. When the base of the pot gets warm, add the shrimp and cook, covered, stirring frequently for about 4 minutes until the shrimp turn pink. Remove from pot and set aside.

2 Stir the marinara into the pot and cover. When the mixture starts to boil, add the red chili, stir well, and allow to simmer until sauce slightly reduces, stirring occasionally.

3 Switch to Warm, add the cooked pasta, and mix well.

4 Before serving, dish out the pasta onto serving plates and top it with cooked shrimp. Garnish with the oregano.

Easy Shrimp and Celery Pasta Salad

Fresh large tomatoes can be substituted for the cherry tomatoes in this recipe. Slice large tomatoes into smaller wedges so they can be tossed easily in the salad. If that's not quite easy enough, go with cherry or grape tomatoes as described here.

Serves 2

4 cups water

12 medium shrimp, peeled and deveined

2 teaspoons grated ginger

4 cups water

½ pound fusilli, cooked

1 celery stalk, finely shredded

4 cherry tomatoes, cut into quarters

½ teaspoon sesame oil

¼ teaspoon ground black pepper

¼ teaspoon ground white pepper

1 green onion, finely chopped, for garnish

1   Season the shrimp with the ginger and place in the rice cooker's steamer basket. Add the water to the pot, cover, and set to Cook.

2   When the water boils, place the shrimp in the cooker, cover, and steam until the shrimp turn pink and cook through, about 7 minutes. Remove and set aside.

3   Add the cooked pasta, shrimp, celery, tomatoes, sesame oil, and black and white pepper together in a large bowl. Mix well, then separate into serving bowls. Garnish with the green onions before serving.

Lentil Soup with Pasta

If you use dried lentils, be sure to cook them in stock until they become tender before beginning this recipe. That process usually takes about an hour, sometimes longer. Canned lentils are more convenient when you want to whip up this dish in less than 30 minutes.

Serves 4

8 cups water

2 teaspoons plus ¼ teaspoon salt, divided

½ pound pasta, preferably shell or bowtie pasta

1 tablespoon extra-virgin olive oil

1 tablespoon finely chopped bacon

½ cup finely chopped onions

2 cloves garlic, peeled and finely minced

1 celery stalk, finely chopped

1 cup canned lentils, drained

6 cups Vegetable or Chicken Stock (see Chapter 2)

¼ teaspoon ground black pepper

1 Add the water to the pot, cover, and set to Cook. When the water comes to a boil, add 2 teaspoons salt and pasta. Stir the pasta gently to prevent it from sticking to the base of the pot. Cover and allow pasta to cook for about 6 minutes. The pasta should be slightly undercooked. Dish it out, drain, and set it aside.

2 Clean out the rice cooker and wipe dry. Add the oil to the pot, cover, and set to Cook. When the base of the pot gets warm, add the bacon, onions, garlic, and celery and cook for about 5 minutes until onions are soft and bacon begins to brown, covered and stirring frequently. Add the partially cooked pasta and stir to coat it with the bacon mixture. Add the lentils and stock and cover. Bring the mixture to a boil.

3 Switch the rice cooker to Warm and simmer for 8 minutes or until the pasta is fully cooked. Add ¼ teaspoon salt and pepper. Ladle pasta with soup into serving bowls.

Al Dente Pasta

When is pasta al dente? *Al dente* means the pasta is firm yet tender, but the only way to tell if the pasta is correctly cooked to the texture you prefer is to taste it while you're cooking.

Spicy Italian Sausage Pasta

What makes a sausage Italian? In the US, an Italian sausage is usually a pork or turkey sausage seasoned with anise and fennel. An Italian sausage becomes sweet when it is flecked with basil and spicy when sprinkled with red pepper flakes.

Serves 2

1 tablespoon extra-virgin olive oil
½ cup finely chopped onions
1 clove garlic, peeled and finely minced
3 spicy Italian sausages, cut into bite-sized pieces
½ (14½-ounce) can diced tomatoes, with juice
½ pound fusilli, cooked
3 cups fresh baby spinach

1 Add the oil to the rice cooker, cover, and set to Cook. When the base gets warm, add the onions and garlic and cook for about 4 minutes until onions turn slightly soft.

2 Add sausage, cover, and cook for about 4 minutes, stirring occasionally.

3 Stir in the tomatoes and continue to cook for 1 minute covered, then uncover and cook for an additional 1 minute.

4 Add the cooked pasta and mix well. Switch rice cooker to Warm and add the spinach. Serve warm.

Lemon Pasta

This dish can be served warm or cold, and cold lemon dishes, not common in American cuisine, can be a cool, tart surprise for that very reason. This one's light and refreshing and makes a wonderful dish for a hot summer day.

Serves 2

2 tablespoons extra-virgin olive oil

2 cloves garlic, peeled and finely minced

1 teaspoon grated ginger

½ teaspoon red pepper flakes

3 tablespoons lemon juice

2 tablespoons water

½ teaspoon salt

½ teaspoon ground black pepper

½ pound thin-strand pasta, cooked

Zest of half a lemon, for garnish

¼ cup finely chopped fresh cilantro, for garnish

1 Add the oil to the pot, cover, and set to Cook. When the base gets warm, add the garlic, ginger, and red pepper flakes and cook covered for 3 minutes. Uncover and cook 3 minutes more or until fragrant. Transfer the mixture to a serving bowl.

2 Add the lemon juice and water to the garlic and oil mixture and whisk to combine into a dressing. Season with the salt and black pepper.

3 Add the pasta and toss well with the dressing. Garnish with lemon zest and cilantro.

Mushroom Pasta

This dish is full of earthy flavors thanks to all the mushrooms. Choose a Chinese vegetable like bok choy or choy sum, blanch and shock it (as described in the recipe in this chapter for Chicken and Shrimp Pasta), and toss it into the final dish.

Serves 2

- 2 tablespoons extra-virgin olive oil
- 3 medium shallots, peeled and thinly sliced
- 4 fresh shiitake mushroom caps, thinly sliced
- 1 cup thinly sliced white mushrooms
- 1 cup thinly sliced brown mushrooms
- 1 (14½-ounce) can diced tomatoes, with juice
- 1 cup water
- ¼ teaspoon salt
- ¼ teaspoon ground black pepper
- ½ pound fusilli, cooked
- ¼ teaspoon dried oregano, for garnish

1 Add the oil to the pot, cover, and set to Cook. When the base of the pot gets warm, add the shallots and cook until slightly soft, about 5 minutes.

2 Add the mushrooms, the tomatoes, and the water. Mix well. Cover the rice cooker and set to Cook.

3 When the sauce mixture starts to simmer, switch to Warm and continue to simmer for 12 minutes or until the mushrooms become tender.

4 Add the salt, pepper, and cooked pasta and mix well. Garnish with oregano before serving.

Pasta and Tuna Salad

Once a quintessential Mediterranean dish, pasta and tuna salad has gone global. If you usually make this dish with a different type of pasta, start making it with the farfalle or bowtie pasta as outlined here—the noodle doesn't dominate the dish but blends right in to the bite.

Serves 2

- 1 tablespoon finely chopped bacon
- 1 cup finely diced green beans
- 1 cup diced cherry tomatoes
- ½ pound bowtie pasta, cooked
- 1 tablespoon extra-virgin olive oil
- 1 tablespoon lemon juice
- ¼ cup finely chopped fresh cilantro
- ¼ teaspoon salt
- ¼ teaspoon ground black pepper
- 1 cup canned flaked tuna

1 Turn the rice cooker to Cook. When the base of the pot gets warm, add the bacon, green beans, and tomatoes. Cook for about 5 minutes, covered and stirring frequently, until green beans are tender and bacon begins to brown. Dish out into a serving bowl.

2 Combine cooked pasta with the green bean mixture.

3 In a small bowl, combine the olive oil, lemon juice, cilantro, salt, and pepper and stir to mix. Pour the dressing over the pasta. Top with tuna and serve.

Asian Noodle Dishes

Save your money and save your health from the added MSG and fatty oils from those cute little takeout boxes. Your rice cooker will yield a variety of tasty noodles by steaming the flavors in this one-pot wonder. Asian flavors are very popular due to the balance of sweet and sour and spicy and umami left on your tongue. From Chilled Soba in Green Onion Dressing and Chicken Mushroom Noodles to Tom Yum Glass Noodles and Udon in Spiced Cauliflower, the collection of recipes in this chapter will have you and your family slurping noodles for months. And if you miss eating with wooden chopsticks out of those white and red boxes, they can be purchased at specialty stores and online.

Chilled Soba in Green Onion Dressing

Buckwheat, which is often used in Japan to make traditional buckwheat soba noodles, is tasty served hot or chilled, and healthy both ways too. It's loaded with B vitamins, and for the wheat-intolerant, it contains no gluten.

Serves 2

1 tablespoon water, for the dressing
1 tablespoon soy sauce
½ teaspoon mirin or other rice wine
1 teaspoon sesame oil
½ cup finely chopped green onions
6 cups water, for cooking rice
½ pound dried soba noodles
8–10 cups cold water with ice, for cold-water bath
2 tablespoons toasted sesame seeds

1 In a small bowl, combine 1 tablespoon water, soy sauce, mirin, and sesame oil. Ladle the dressing into 2 serving bowls, then add the green onions.

2 Add the 6 cups water to the rice cooker, cover, and set to Cook. When the water boils, add noodles and stir gently to prevent sticking. Cook for 6 minutes.

3 Drain the noodles and plunge them into the cold-water bath for 4 minutes.

4 Place the noodles in the serving bowls containing the dressing and toss to combine. Garnish with toasted sesame seeds before serving.

Warm Soba and Japanese Mushrooms in Ginger Dressing

Be sure to use enough unsalted boiling water for cooking dried soba noodles. If you don't add enough water, your noodles will become starchy and sticky. Be careful not to overcook; soba noodles don't stand up to overcooking as well as other noodles do.

Serves 2

- 2 teaspoons grated ginger
- 1 tablespoon finely chopped green onions
- 1 teaspoon soy sauce
- 1 teaspoon sesame oil
- 2 tablespoons water, for dressing
- 6 cups water, for cooking rice
- 1 (3½-ounce) pack Japanese beech (shimeji) mushrooms
- ½ pound dried soba noodles

1 In a medium bowl, combine ginger, green onions, soy sauce, sesame oil, and 2 tablespoons water. Ladle half the dressing into serving bowls. Set the remaining half aside to dress the mushrooms.

2 Add the 6 cups of water to the rice cooker, cover, and set to Cook. When the water boils, add the mushrooms and blanch for 20 seconds until the mushrooms are tender. Dish out the mushrooms and place in the medium bowl with the remaining dressing. Toss well to coat the mushrooms.

3 Cover the rice cooker again and return the water to a boil. Add the noodles, stirring gently to prevent sticking to the base of the pot. Allow noodles to cook for 5 minutes or until cooked to taste.

4 Drain the noodles and divide among the serving bowls containing the dressing. Toss to combine. Top the noodles with the mushrooms and serve warm.

Kimchi Soba Soup

In Korea, kimchi is almost any dish made with pickled vegetables. In the United States and most of the world, it refers to the familiar napa cabbage and radish concoction that has exploded in popularity over the past two decades.

Serves 4

12 cups water, divided
½ pound dried soba noodles
½ block soft tofu (about 5 ounces), cut into ½-inch cubes
1 cup finely shredded kimchi
1 nori sheet (Japanese seaweed), shredded

1 Add 6 cups water to the rice cooker, cover, and set to Cook. When the water boils, add noodles and stir gently. Cook for 5 minutes or more to taste. Drain the noodles and set aside in serving bowls.

2 Clean out the rice cooker and wipe dry. Add 6 cups water to the pot, cover, and set to Cook. When the water boils, add the tofu, switch the rice cooker to Warm, and simmer for 3 minutes.

3 Stir in kimchi and simmer for another 3 minutes. Ladle over noodles and serve. Garnish with nori.

Sea Vegetables

Similar to kelp, nori is considered a sea vegetable. Sea vegetables contain a wide range of minerals such as iodine, vitamin K, folate, iron, and calcium.

Summer Soba with Spinach and Mushrooms

Try this recipe with cha soba, a popular summer soba variety. They're soba noodles with a light-green tinge, which comes from the green tea powder added to the buckwheat flour mix, and they really do come out tasting like tea!

Serves 2

2 cups warm water, for the dressing

3 tablespoons soy sauce

1 tablespoon mirin

1 teaspoon grated ginger

1 teaspoon sesame oil

6 cups water, for cooking rice

3 tightly packed cups fresh baby spinach

1 cup thinly sliced fresh shiitake mushroom caps

½ pound dried soba noodles

8–10 cups water with ice, for cold-water bath

1 In a medium bowl, add the warm water, soy sauce, mirin, ginger, and sesame oil and stir to combine. Chill the dressing in the refrigerator for about 1 hour.

2 Add 6 cups water to the rice cooker, cover, and set to Cook. When the water boils, add the spinach and blanch for 10 seconds. Remove spinach from pot and set aside to cool.

3 Place the mushrooms in the water and blanch for 15–20 seconds until the mushrooms are tender. Remove from pot and set aside to cool.

4 Cover the rice cooker again and return the water to a boil. Add the noodles, stirring gently to prevent sticking. Allow noodles to cook for 5 minutes or more until done to taste.

5 Drain the noodles and plunge them into the cold-water bath for 3–5 minutes. Drain and set aside in serving bowls. Top the noodles with the spinach and mushrooms and serve with the chilled dressing on the side as a dipping sauce.

Udon in Spiced Cauliflower

We call for fresh udon in this dish, but you may need to work with dried noodles, and that's fine. Typically, dried udon is boiled for about 10 minutes. The noodles should be *koshi*—tender with no hard core, and the noodle surface should be slippery yet not overly soft.

Serves 4

- 6 cups water, divided
- 1 pound cauliflower florets
- 2 (7-ounce) packs fresh udon
- 1 tablespoon butter, divided
- 2 medium shallots, peeled and thinly sliced
- 2 cloves garlic, peeled and finely minced
- 1 teaspoon grated ginger
- ½ teaspoon cumin seeds
- ¼ teaspoon mustard seeds
- ½ tablespoon curry powder
- ½ teaspoon turmeric
- ¼ teaspoon salt
- ¼ teaspoon ground black pepper
- ¼ teaspoon red pepper flakes
- 1 tablespoon finely chopped fresh cilantro

1. Add 5 cups water to the rice cooker, cover, and set to Cook. When the water boils, add the cauliflower florets and blanch for 30 seconds. Without draining the cooking water, remove florets and set aside to cool.

2. Cover the rice cooker and return the water to a boil. When boiling, add noodles to blanch. Stir gently to prevent sticking to the base of the pot. Allow noodles to cook until noodles are separated, about 2 minutes. Drain the noodles and set aside.

3. Clean out the rice cooker and wipe dry. Add ½ tablespoon of the butter to the rice cooker, cover, and set to Cook. When the base of the rice cooker gets warm, add the shallots and cook until they begin to soften, about 5 minutes.

4. Add the garlic, ginger, cumin, and mustard seeds and cook until fragrant, about 5 minutes.

5. Stir in the cauliflower, curry powder, turmeric, and the remaining 1 cup water. Cover and return to a boil.

6. Add the remaining ½ tablespoon butter, salt and black pepper, and red pepper flakes. Stir well, cover, and allow mixture to simmer on Warm for about 10 minutes.

7. One minute before serving, add the cilantro and mix well. Add the noodles and cauliflower mixture to a deep bowl and toss gently before serving.

Black Pepper Chicken Noodles

Udon noodles have a firmer texture than soba noodles and are better for stir-fries. But that distinctive texture is lost if the noodles are in boiling water much more than a minute.

Serves 3

- 1 teaspoon oyster sauce
- 1 teaspoon soy sauce
- ½ teaspoon brown sugar
- 1¼ teaspoons ground black pepper, divided
- 7 cups water, divided
- 2 (7-ounce) packs fresh udon noodles
- 3 tablespoons vegetable oil
- 1 medium onion, peeled and thinly sliced
- 2 cloves garlic, peeled and finely minced
- 1 teaspoon grated ginger
- 1 chicken breast or thigh, sliced into thin strips
- 3 tightly packed cups shredded round or napa cabbage
- ¼ teaspoon salt

1. In a small bowl, combine oyster sauce, soy sauce, brown sugar, 1 teaspoon pepper, and 1 cup water. Stir well and set aside as gravy mixture.

2. Add 5 cups water to the rice cooker, cover, and set to Cook. When the water boils, add the noodles to blanch. Blanch noodles for about 1 minute until noodles are separated. Drain the noodles and set aside.

3. Clean out the rice cooker and wipe dry. Add the oil to the rice cooker, cover, and set to Cook. When the base of the rice cooker gets warm, add the onions and cook about 5 minutes until slightly soft.

4. Add garlic and ginger and cook covered about 5 minutes until fragrant, stirring frequently. Add chicken and cabbage and cook for 3–5 minutes until chicken browns. Remove from pot and set aside, leaving the remaining oil in the rice cooker.

5. Add the prepared gravy mixture to the pot, cover rice cooker, and cook for 1–2 minutes until mixture bubbles.

6. Return the cabbage and chicken mixture to the gravy, stir in remaining 1 cup water, and cook for 2–3 minutes until chicken cooks through, switching down to Warm if gravy mixture bubbles too vigorously.

7. When sauce reduces and thickens, add the udon noodles and toss well with the gravy. Add the salt and remaining ¼ teaspoon pepper. If you haven't already, switch the rice cooker to Warm and allow noodles to simmer until they absorb most of the gravy. Serve warm.

Beef and Mushroom Fried Noodles

Yaki udon is stir-fried udon in a soy-based sauce. This recipe uses ground beef and mushrooms as the main ingredients, inspired by Japanese teppanyaki. Try a variety of mushrooms to add depth to the stir-fry!

Serves 2

5½ cups water, divided

2 (7-ounce) packs fresh udon

2 tablespoons vegetable oil

½ pound ground beef

1 (3½-ounce) pack Japanese beech mushrooms

1 (½-inch) piece fresh ginger, thinly shredded

1 teaspoon soy sauce

2 green onions, sliced into finger-length pieces

¼ tablespoon salt

¼ tablespoon ground black pepper

1   Add 5 cups water to the rice cooker, cover, and set to Cook. When the water boils, add the noodles to blanch. Stirring gently to prevent sticking, blanch for about 1 minute until noodles are separated. Drain the noodles and set aside.

2   Clean out the rice cooker and wipe dry. Add oil to the rice cooker, cover, and set to Cook. When the base gets warm, add the beef, mushrooms, ginger, and soy sauce and cook for 4–5 minutes until the beef begins to turn brown.

3   Add remaining ½ cup water, cover, and continue to cook for about 8 minutes. When the mixture starts to simmer, add the udon noodles, the green onions, and the salt and pepper and toss well.

4   Switch the rice cooker to Warm and simmer noodles until they absorb the sauce. Serve warm.

Rice Noodles with Beef

Rice stick noodles tend to stick together during stir-frying, and it may be hard to separate the strands in the rice cooker. Whether the noodles are fresh or dried, soak them in warm water before cooking to soften and loosen up the strands.

Serves 2

2 tablespoons vegetable oil

½ pound ground beef

1 clove garlic, peeled and finely minced

1 tablespoon black bean paste

¼ pound broccoli florets, blanched

2 tablespoons water

½ pound dried rice stick noodles, soaked in warm water for 10 minutes or until softened

1 tablespoon soy sauce

2 green onions, thinly sliced, divided

1 Add the oil to the rice cooker, cover, and set to Cook. When the base of the rice cooker gets warm, add the ground beef and cook for 10 minutes until the beef completely cooks through, covered and stirring occasionally. Leaving the remaining oil in the pot, remove the beef from the pot and set aside.

2 Add the garlic, black bean paste, broccoli, and water to the pot and cook for 3 minutes until vegetables are tender.

3 Add the noodles, soy sauce, and half the green onions. Mix well.

4 Return the beef to the pot and mix well with the noodles. Garnish with remaining green onions before serving.

Tom Yum Glass Noodles

Glass noodles are known by many names. You may have heard them called bean noodles, bean vermicelli, or even just plain clear noodles. As you probably guessed, glass noodles are so-called because of their translucent appearance when cooked.

Serves 2

7 cups water, divided

2 small bunches bok choy

2 tablespoons vegetable oil

2 medium shallots, peeled and thinly sliced

1 lemongrass stalk, bruised bottom half and white part chopped

¼ pound ground pork

1 teaspoon tom yum paste

4 medium shrimp, peeled and deveined

4 ounces firm tofu, cut into ½-inch cubes

¼ pound glass noodles, soaked in warm water for 10 minutes or until softened

1 Add 4 cups water to the rice cooker, cover, and set to Cook. When the water boils, add the bok choy and blanch for 20 seconds or until tender. Remove from pot and set aside.

2 Clean out the rice cooker and wipe dry. Add the oil, cover, and set to Cook. When the base gets warm, add the shallots and lemongrass and cook for about 5 minutes until fragrant.

3 Add the ground pork and tom yum paste and cook for 6 minutes, covering intermittently.

4 Add 3 cups water to the cooker, cover, and allow to boil. When boiling, add the shrimp and tofu, cover, and simmer for 5 minutes or until shrimp turn pink. Remove the shrimp using kitchen tongs and set aside.

5 Add the glass noodles into the tom yum mixture, cover rice cooker, and allow to come to a simmer. Once simmering, immediately dish out glass noodles into serving bowls, top noodles with shrimp and bok choy, and ladle remaining soup over noodles. Serve immediately.

Glass Noodles

Glass noodles absorb moisture like a sponge. Don't simmer them for too long in a soup base or they will absorb too much liquid and turn soft and mushy.

Stir-Fry Glass Noodles with Mushrooms and Celery

It's easy to confuse glass noodles, which are typically made from mung beans, with rice vermicelli, which of course is rice based. Some cooks aren't confused but try to substitute one for the other anyway. Don't! They look a bit alike but otherwise have little in common.

Serves 2

- 1 teaspoon oyster sauce
- 1 teaspoon soy sauce
- ½ teaspoon sugar
- 2 cups water, divided
- 2 tablespoons vegetable oil
- 2 cloves garlic, peeled and finely minced
- 2 cups diced brown cremini mushrooms
- 1 celery stalk, diced
- ½ teaspoon each salt, ground black pepper, and ground white pepper
- ¼ pound glass noodles, soaked in warm water for 10 minutes or until softened
- 1 teaspoon finely chopped fresh cilantro, for garnish

1 Mix oyster sauce, soy sauce, sugar, and 1 cup of the water in a small bowl. Set aside as sauce.

2 Add the oil to the rice cooker, cover, and set to Cook. When the base is warm, add the garlic, then the mushrooms and celery. Cook about 5 minutes until fragrant, covered and stirring occasionally.

3 Add the sauce mixture, cover, and cook until slightly bubbling. Add remaining cup of water, cover, and simmer the mixture for about 5 minutes, switching to Warm if mixture bubbles too vigorously.

4 Add the salt and black and white pepper. Add the glass noodles, mix well, and allow noodles to absorb the sauce mixture.

5 Ladle into serving bowls and garnish with cilantro before serving.

Pork-Mushroom Noodles

This dish is very similar to a popular noodle dish sold from carts in the streets of Singapore. Try to use flat egg noodles if you can find them, but other kinds of Chinese noodles will do in a pinch: rice noodles like *ho fun* are a good substitute.

Serves 2

1 tablespoon soy sauce

1 teaspoon oyster sauce

1 teaspoon brown sugar

4 cups water, divided

½ pound dried Chinese noodles

2 tablespoons vegetable oil

1 clove garlic, peeled and finely minced

½ pound ground pork

2 medium shallots, peeled and thinly sliced

6 fresh shiitake mushroom caps, thinly sliced

¼ teaspoon ground white pepper

¼ teaspoon salt

1 tablespoon balsamic vinegar, or more as preferred

1. For the sauce, mix the soy sauce, oyster sauce, sugar, and 1 cup water in a bowl and set aside.

2. Add remaining 3 cups water to the rice cooker, cover, and set to Cook. When the water boils, add the noodles and stir gently to prevent sticking. Allow noodles to cook for 8 minutes or more until done to taste. Drain the noodles and set aside.

3. Clean out the rice cooker and wipe dry. Add the oil to the rice cooker, cover, and set to Cook. When the base warms, add the garlic and cook about 5 minutes until fragrant.

4. Add the pork and cook about 8 minutes until the pork browns, covered and stirring occasionally. Dish out the pork and set aside.

5. Add the shallots and mushrooms and cook 2–3 minutes until shallots are soft. Add the sauce mixture, cover, and allow to come to a slight simmer. Switch to Warm and continue to simmer until mushrooms are soft, about 10 minutes.

6. Return the pork to the rice cooker and continue to simmer on Warm for 15 minutes or until pork cooks through. Add the pepper and salt and drizzle 1 tablespoon balsamic vinegar into the mixture during the last 2 minutes of cooking.

7. Add the noodles to the rice cooker and mix well with the ground meat mixture. Add more balsamic vinegar if desired and mix well with the noodles.

Spicy Bean Noodles

If you can't find dried Chinese noodles in supermarkets near you, substitute instant Chinese noodles. Cook the instant noodles according to package instructions and set aside in serving bowls.

Serves 3

7 cups water, divided

½ pound dried Chinese noodles or 3 (3-ounce) packs dried instant noodles

2 tablespoons vegetable oil

¼ pound ground pork

1 clove garlic, peeled and finely minced

1 green onion, finely chopped

1 tablespoon hot chili bean paste (Lee Kum Kee, etc.)

1 cup finely shredded cucumber, drained of excess moisture, for garnish

1 Add 5 cups water to the rice cooker, cover, and set to Cook. When the water boils, add the noodles and stir gently to prevent sticking. Cover rice cooker and allow noodles to cook for about 3 minutes; refer to packet instructions as a guide. Drain the noodles and set aside in serving bowls.

2 Clean out the rice cooker and wipe dry. Add the oil, cover, and set to Cook. When the base warms, add the ground pork and cook, covered, stirring occasionally for 5 minutes or until pork is browned. Dish out the pork and set aside. Leave the remaining oil in the pot.

3 Add the garlic, green onions, and bean paste to the pot and continue cooking for 2 minutes. Add remaining 2 cups water, cover, and bring to a simmer.

4 Return the pork to the rice cooker and simmer on Warm for 15 minutes or until pork cooks through.

5 Ladle the sauce over the noodles and garnish with cucumber before serving.

Noodles in Creamy Egg Gravy

For creamy and smooth egg gravy over savory dishes, avoid cooking eggs over high heat, either in the rice cooker or in a pan on the stovetop. Turn down the heat and stir in the whisked egg slowly, using a chopstick to stir the eggs in one direction.

Serves 2

6 cups water

½ pound dried Chinese noodles

2 tablespoons vegetable oil

6 medium shrimp, peeled, deveined, and cut into bite-sized pieces

2 cloves garlic, peeled and finely minced

1 teaspoon grated ginger

¼ pound sliced chicken thigh meat, about ¼-inch thick

4 fresh shiitake mushroom caps, diced

1 cup broccoli florets, blanched

½ tablespoon oyster sauce

2 cups hot water

¼ teaspoon ground white pepper

¼ teaspoon salt

1 egg, lightly whisked

1 Add 6 cups water to the rice cooker, cover, and set to Cook. When the water boils, add the noodles and stir gently to prevent sticking to the base of the pot. Cover and cook for about 5 minutes. Drain the noodles and set aside in serving bowls.

2 Clean out the rice cooker and wipe dry. Add the oil to the rice cooker, cover, and set to Cook. When the base warms, add the shrimp and cook about 8 minutes until shrimp turn pink. Leaving the remaining oil in the pot, dish out shrimp and set aside.

3 Add the garlic, ginger, and chicken to the pot. Cook covered for about 8 minutes until the chicken pieces brown on the surface, stirring occasionally.

4 Add the mushrooms, broccoli, oyster sauce, and 2 cups hot water. Stir, cover, and allow mixture to come to a simmer.

5 Switch to Warm and continue to simmer for about 8 minutes until chicken cooks through. Stir the shrimp into the pot. Season with pepper and salt. Slowly add the whisked egg, swirling gently in one direction using a chopstick. The heat remaining in the mixture will cook the egg to a smooth consistency. Ladle the mixture on top of the noodles and serve.

Stir-Fry White Pepper Noodles

You can substitute rice vermicelli for the noodles in this dish. Before using the vermicelli, soak in warm water to soften it. In this as in any other rice vermicelli dish, that's all the cooking these handy noodles need!

Serves 2

- 1 teaspoon oyster sauce
- 2 teaspoons soy sauce, divided
- 2 tablespoons warm water
- 1/4 pound thin pork slices, about 1/4-inch thick
- 1/4 teaspoon plus 1/2 teaspoon ground white pepper, divided
- 1 teaspoon Chinese cooking wine
- 5 cups water
- 1/2 pound dried Chinese noodles (thicker strands preferred)
- 2 tablespoons vegetable oil
- 3 medium shallots, peeled and thinly sliced
- 2 cloves garlic, peeled and finely minced
- 1 pound round or napa cabbage, thinly shredded
- 1 medium carrot, peeled and thinly shredded
- 1 cup Vegetable Stock (see Chapter 2)
- 1/2 teaspoon salt
- 1 tablespoon finely chopped fresh cilantro, for garnish

1. For the sauce, add the oyster sauce, 1 teaspoon soy sauce, and warm water to a small bowl and whisk to combine. Set aside.

2. In a medium bowl, add the pork, 1 teaspoon soy sauce, 1/4 teaspoon pepper, and Chinese cooking wine and stir to combine; set aside to marinate in the refrigerator.

3. Add 5 cups water to the rice cooker, cover, and set to Cook. When the water boils, add the noodles and stir gently to prevent sticking. Allow noodles to cook until al dente, about 3 minutes. Drain the noodles and set aside.

4. Clean out the rice cooker and wipe dry. Add the oil, cover, and set to Cook. When the base of the rice cooker gets warm, add the pork and cook for about 8 minutes until browned. Leave the remaining oil in the pot; remove pork and set aside.

5. Add the shallots and garlic to the pot and cook about 5 minutes until shallots are slightly soft. Add the cabbage and carrots and mix well. Cover and cook for 5 minutes or until the vegetables are tender.

6. Add the sauce mixture, stock, and the pork. Mix well, cover, and allow to come to simmer. Once simmering, add the salt, switch rice cooker to Warm, and simmer for 8 minutes.

7. Add the cooked noodles and remaining 1/2 teaspoon pepper. Mix well and allow to simmer covered for about 6 minutes until gravy reduces. Garnish with cilantro and serve.

Nyonya-Style Noodles

This noodle dish is a Peranakan favorite. In Peranakan culture (Peranakans are the mixed-race people of Indonesia, Malaysia, and Singapore) *nyonya* refers to the female descendants of early Chinese immigrants. The reason for the name is lost to us, but one imagines that among those early Chinese ladies were some very good cooks!

Serves 2

6 cups water

¼ pound fresh yellow noodles (round and fat noodles preferred)

2 tablespoons vegetable oil

2 cloves garlic, peeled and finely minced

½ tablespoon mashed fermented salted soy beans

½ pound shredded napa cabbage

6–8 medium shrimp, peeled and deveined

¼ pound rice vermicelli, softened in warm water

¼ pound fresh mung bean sprouts

3 cups Shrimp Stock (see Chapter 2)

¼ teaspoon salt

¼ teaspoon ground white pepper

1 tablespoon finely chopped green onions, for garnish

1. Add the water to the rice cooker, cover, and set to Cook. When the water boils, add the noodles to blanch. Stir gently to prevent sticking. Blanch for about 1 minute until noodles are separated. Drain the noodles and set aside.

2. Clean out the rice cooker and wipe dry. Add the oil, cover, and set to Cook. When the base of the rice cooker gets warm, add the garlic and mashed soy beans and cook for about 5 minutes until fragrant.

3. Add the cabbage and shrimp and cook until vegetables become slightly soft and shrimp turn pink, about 6 minutes.

4. Add the yellow noodles, rice vermicelli, bean sprouts, and the Shrimp Stock. Mix well, cover, and simmer for 5 minutes. Switch to Warm and simmer for 8 more minutes. Season with the salt and pepper. Garnish with green onions and serve.

Which Noodles?

The best noodles for this dish are the fresh yellow noodles usually found in the refrigerator section in Asian supermarkets, alongside the wonton wrappers and the tofu. Fresh yellow noodles may be hard to find, in which case you should use spaghetti.

Chicken Mushroom Noodles

The essential difference between mirin, or Japanese rice wine, and the Chinese variety called for here lies in sweetness. Mirin is fermented and could easily be called "sweet rice wine" in English. Chinese rice wine is unfermented and dryer.

Serves 3

½ **pound chicken thighs, sliced into thin strips**

½ **teaspoon soy sauce**

1 **teaspoon Chinese cooking wine**

½ **teaspoon sesame oil**

5 **cups water**

1 **small bundle Chinese broccoli**

3 **packs instant noodle bundles**

2 **tablespoons vegetable oil**

2 **medium shallots, peeled and thinly sliced**

1 **clove garlic, peeled and finely minced**

6 **fresh shiitake mushroom caps, thinly sliced**

2 **cups Chicken Stock (see Chapter 2)**

¼ **teaspoon ground white pepper**

1 In a medium bowl, add the chicken, soy sauce, Chinese cooking wine, and sesame oil and stir to combine; set aside to marinate in the refrigerator.

2 Add the water to the rice cooker, cover, and set to Cook. When the water boils, add the Chinese broccoli and blanch for 30 seconds. Remove broccoli from pot and set aside.

3 Cover the rice cooker and return to a boil. When boiling, add the noodles, stirring gently to prevent sticking. Allow noodles to cook for 5 minutes or until firm yet not overcooked. Drain the noodles and divide them among the serving plates. Top the noodles with the Chinese broccoli.

4 Clean out the rice cooker and wipe dry. Add the oil, cover, and set to Cook. When the base of the rice cooker gets warm, add the shallots and cook for about 3 minutes until slightly soft. Add the garlic and cook for 3 minutes more.

5 Add the marinated chicken and the mushrooms. Mix well and cook for 3 minutes or until chicken browns, covered and stirring occasionally.

6 Add the stock, cover the rice cooker, and allow the mixture to come to a simmer. When simmering, add the pepper, switch to Warm, and simmer for 5 minutes or until chicken cooks through and the sauce slightly thickens.

7 Ladle the chicken and mushroom sauce over the noodles and serve immediately.

Fish and Seafood Main Dishes

Many people order fish and seafood in restaurants but often overlook cooking it in the home. The fear of overcooking those beautiful fillets or dealing with those littleneck clams often lead home cooks to turn to their go-to chicken and beef dishes. Fear no more. The rice cooker allows you to prepare these nutrient-packed, water-dwelling delicacies to steamed perfection. Choose fresh products and use within 1–2 days of purchase for optimal freshness. The recipes in this chapter—from Halibut with Mango Salsa to Creamed Corn Crabcakes and Coconut Poached Cod to Quick Seafood Jambalaya—will make you feel like you are dining alfresco in the salty air overlooking the crashing waves on the beach. And don't forget your margarita. It is the perfect pairing for any beach-worthy meal!

Salmon Fillet with Oyster Sauce

When cooking salmon fillet with the skin on, always cook skin-side down first. Another tip: those white spots you probably often see bubbling up on the skin as it cooks are a natural protein. Some cooks and diners like them; some find them a bit unsightly. To prevent them from forming, just bring your fish all the way up to room temperature before cooking,

Serves 2

1 teaspoon oyster sauce
½ teaspoon brown sugar
1 teaspoon grated ginger
½ teaspoon grated garlic
½ cup water
2 (4-ounce) salmon fillets, about ½-inch thick
¼ teaspoon salt
¼ teaspoon ground white pepper
1 teaspoon corn flour
2 tablespoons vegetable oil
1 tablespoon finely chopped green onions
2 fresh shiitake mushroom caps, thinly sliced

1 Mix the oyster sauce, brown sugar, grated ginger, garlic, and water in a small bowl. Set aside as sauce.

2 Season both sides of the fish with the salt and pepper; pat both sides with the corn flour.

3 Add the oil to the rice cooker, cover, and set to Cook. When the base of the pot gets warm, add the salmon skin-side down and pan-fry the fish on one side, for 4 minutes covered until fish turns pinkish-orange. Leaving the remaining oil in the pot, remove salmon and set aside.

4 Add the green onions and mushroom slices. Stir in the prepared sauce, cover the rice cooker, and allow to simmer for 1 minute.

5 Return the fish to the pot, cover the rice cooker, and allow to simmer for another 1 minute or until sauce thickens slightly and fish completely cooks through.

Halibut with Mango Salsa

Halibut tends to have a naturally sweet flavor and, even better, lacks a "fishy" smell. It doesn't need much seasoning as a result and pairs very well with this or any light, subtle sauce that won't overpower the fish itself.

Serves 2

- 2 (¾-pound) halibut fillets, cut into ¼-inch-thick slices
- ½ teaspoon salt
- ½ teaspoon ground black pepper
- 1 teaspoon corn flour
- 1 cup ripe cubed mango
- ½ cup cubed kiwi
- ¼ cup finely chopped fresh cilantro
- ¼ cup thinly sliced shallots
- 1 tablespoon lime juice
- 3 tablespoons extra-virgin olive oil
- 2 tablespoons chopped parsley leaves

1 Season the fish with the salt and pepper and coat lightly with corn flour.

2 Mix together the mango, kiwi, cilantro, shallots, and lime juice in a small bowl. Chill in the refrigerator.

3 Add the oil to the rice cooker, cover, and set to Cook. When the base of the pot gets warm and working in batches if necessary, add the fish pieces in a single layer across the pot. Cook each side for about 3 minutes covered until fish cooks through. Keep the first batches warm while the rest of the fish is cooking.

4 Transfer fish slices to a serving plate and spoon the mango salsa over the top. Garnish with parsley and serve.

Fish in Creamy Pistachio Pesto Sauce

Use pine nuts or cashew nuts as alternatives to pistachios. The pesto in this recipe may yield more than you'll need for the sauce. Whatever's left over will keep in the refrigerator for 2 weeks and doubles as a great dressing.

Serves 2

1 cup fresh basil

½ cup shelled pistachios

2 cloves garlic, peeled

½ cup grated Parmesan cheese

3 tablespoons extra-virgin olive oil, divided

2 (5-ounce) firm whitefish fillets (sole, snapper, or tilapia), about ½-inch thick

¼ teaspoon salt

¼ teaspoon ground black pepper

1 tablespoon butter

½ cup whole milk

1 teaspoon all-purpose flour

1 Add the basil, pistachios, garlic, and cheese to a blender or food processor and process until uniformly chopped. Gradually add 2 tablespoons of the olive oil until the mix reaches a grainy texture. Set aside.

2 Season both sides of the fish with the salt and pepper. Set aside.

3 Add the butter and the remaining olive oil to the rice cooker pot, cover, and set to Cook. When the base of the pot gets warm, gradually stir in the milk and flour. Cover the rice cooker and allow to simmer, switching the cooker to Warm if the mixture boils vigorously.

4 Add the fish, switch back to the Cook setting if necessary, cover the pot, and allow the fish to simmer in the sauce for about 5 minutes until cooked through; the fish should be opaque, white, and firm to the touch. If the sauce bubbles too vigorously, switch to Warm and continue to simmer for the remaining time until the fish cooks through and the sauce thickens.

5 Stir in 1 tablespoon of prepared pesto sauce.

6 Transfer the fish to a serving plate and pour the creamy pesto sauce over fish. Serve immediately.

Whitefish Burgers

This is a quick and easy meal to make, but an even quicker way is to rub some extra-virgin olive oil on the fish, wrap and seal tightly in foil, and steam for about 8 minutes in the rice cooker. Remember to drain the extra moisture from the steamed fish before putting in the burger.

Serves 2

- 2 (5-ounce) firm whitefish fillets (sole, snapper, sea bass) about ½-inch thick
- ¼ teaspoon salt
- ½ teaspoon ground black pepper
- 1 teaspoon turmeric
- 1 teaspoon corn flour
- 2 sesame seed buns, split in half
- 2 teaspoons butter, divided
- 1 tablespoon extra-virgin olive oil
- 2 slices Cheddar or Swiss cheese
- 1 cup alfalfa sprouts

1. If the fish fillets are too long for the buns, slice each fillet in half. Season both sides of the fish with the salt, pepper, and turmeric and pat both sides with corn flour. Set aside.

2. Cover the rice cooker and set to Cook. When the base is warm, place the buns in the cooker split-side down and "toast" for about 1 minute. Remove and set aside.

3. Add 1 teaspoon of the butter and the olive oil to the rice cooker, cover, and set to Cook. When the base of the pot gets warm, add the fillets, cover, and cook on each side for 4 minutes or until cooked through.

4. Meanwhile, use the remaining 1 teaspoon of butter to slightly butter one half of each bun. Place a slice of cheese on each bun; arrange alfalfa sprouts on the cheese.

5. Remove fish from the rice cooker, place on the prepared buns, and serve.

Herb and Garlic Shrimp

For a healthier variation, use extra-virgin olive oil instead of butter. You also can try parsley instead of basil. Whatever you do, make this dish!

Serves 2

1 tablespoon butter

2 cloves garlic, peeled and finely minced

¼ teaspoon salt

¼ teaspoon ground black pepper

1 tablespoon finely chopped fresh basil

1½ tablespoons lemon juice

1 pound medium shrimp, peeled and deveined

1 Add the butter to the rice cooker, cover, and set to Cook. When butter is melted, switch off the rice cooker.

2 In a medium bowl, combine the melted butter, garlic, salt, pepper, basil, lemon juice, and shrimp and stir to mix. Cover and marinate in the refrigerator for 30 minutes.

3 Switch rice cooker to Cook. When the base of the pot gets warm, add the shrimp mixture and cook for about 6 minutes until shrimp cook through.

Coconut Poached Cod

Seafood can be intimidating to home cooks, but now you can let your rice cooker steam those worries away. It can produce juicy, flavorful fish in just minutes, and once you're done, the one-pot cleanup is much easier than just about any other fish preparation out there.

Serves 6

1 (13½-ounce) can coconut milk

1 tablespoon lime juice

1 teaspoon lime zest

1 tablespoon soy sauce

1 teaspoon salt

Pinch cayenne pepper

6 (5-ounce) cod fillets

¼ cup julienned fresh basil

1 In a medium bowl, add the coconut milk, lime juice, lime zest, soy sauce, salt, and cayenne and whisk to combine. Pour into rice cooker pot. Place cod in liquid. Cover and set to Cook.

2 When the liquid starts to boil, reduce heat to Warm and allow to cook for 10 minutes.

3 Transfer fish to a serving dish and spoon a few tablespoons of coconut milk mixture over fillets. Garnish with fresh basil and serve warm.

Shrimp and Tomato Fried Eggs

You'll be tempted to wash your rice cooker after preparing the eggs just as you usually do. It's really not necessary here; in fact, it improves the texture of the dish if you leave some bits and pieces of the egg in the cooker when moving on to the next step.

Serves 4

- 3 large eggs
- ½ teaspoon ground white pepper, divided
- ½ teaspoon salt, divided
- 2 drops sesame oil
- 1 teaspoon Chinese cooking wine
- ½ pound medium shrimp, peeled and deveined
- 4 tablespoons vegetable oil, divided
- 1 medium tomato, thinly sliced
- 2 tablespoons water
- 2 green onions, finely chopped, for garnish

1 Lightly whisk the eggs in a small bowl; add ¼ teaspoon pepper, ¼ teaspoon salt, and sesame oil and stir to combine. Set aside.

2 In a separate bowl, combine ¼ teaspoon salt, ¼ teaspoon pepper, Chinese cooking wine, and shrimp. Set aside to marinate.

3 Add 3 tablespoons of the oil to the rice cooker, cover, and set to Cook. When the base of the pot gets warm, add the egg mixture and cook until egg is just cooked. Immediately remove eggs from pot and set aside.

4 Add the remaining 1 tablespoon oil to the rice cooker, cover, and set to Cook. When the base of the pot gets warm, add the shrimp and cook until shrimp cooks through, about 8 minutes.

5 Add the tomato and stir for 30 seconds. Add the water, then cover rice cooker and allow it to come to a simmer.

6 Uncover and switch the rice cooker to Warm. Return the eggs to the pot and mix well by breaking up the eggs into small pieces. Cook eggs with shrimp and tomatoes for about 4 minutes. Garnish with green onions before serving.

Buttered Scallops

Make sure to cook the scallops in a single layer in the pot, as they release moisture during cooking. If you can't fit all the scallops into the pan base in one batch and need to cook a second batch, give the pot a quick cleaning first.

Serves 2

2 tablespoons butter

8 large scallops, patted dry with paper towels

¼ teaspoon salt

¼ teaspoon ground black pepper

1 tablespoon lemon juice

1. Add the butter to the rice cooker, cover, and set to Cook. When the butter melts and the base of the pot gets warm, add the scallops in a single layer, sprinkle with half the salt and pepper, and cook for 3 minutes.

2. When the scallops begin to turn white, flip them over and sprinkle with remaining salt and pepper. Cook 2 more minutes covered.

3. When scallops become completely white, add the lemon juice and simmer for another minute. Serve warm.

Cooking with Frozen Scallops

Frozen scallops need to be thawed thoroughly before cooking to make sure there is no excess moisture in them. To be sure, set them on paper towels for about 15 minutes prior to cooking.

Clam and Corn in Herb Broth

To safely store clams before cooking them, put them in a colander set inside a large bowl. Place some dampened paper towels over the clams and keep them in the coldest part of your refrigerator. You should use them within a day of purchase.

Serves 4

2 tablespoons olive oil

½ tablespoon butter

3 medium shallots, peeled and thinly sliced

1 teaspoon grated ginger

2 cloves garlic, peeled and finely minced

2 pounds clams

1 cup canned corn kernels, drained

¼ cup dry white wine

¼ teaspoon ground black pepper

½ cup clam stock

1 tablespoon finely chopped fresh basil

1 Add the oil and butter to the rice cooker, cover, and set to Cook. When the base of the pot gets warm, add the shallots and cook for about 3 minutes until soft.

2 Add the ginger and garlic and cook for about 3 minutes until fragrant, covered and stirring occasionally.

3 Add the clams, corn, wine, pepper, and stock. Cover and bring to a simmer. Cook for about 5 minutes, allowing clams to steam until clams show first signs of opening.

4 Continue simmering, removing cover occasionally to check on the clams. Discard any that do not open. Remove the clams that have opened and set them aside in serving bowls.

5 Add the basil to the broth, stir well, and ladle broth over the clams in serving bowls. Serve with crusty bread for dipping into the broth.

How to Cook Clams

Clams open when done; use tongs to remove them and set them aside in a bowl. Overcooked clams are rubbery. If the other ingredients need further cooking, continue to simmer them without the cooked clams. Before serving, ladle the broth over the clams.

Shrimp with Colored Bell Peppers

Adding more color to your diet, as you will when you whip up this colorful dish, can provide health benefits and create a more interesting menu. Red fruits and vegetables such as tomatoes, beets, and red cabbage are packed with antioxidants. Yellow and orange fruits and vegetables contain beta-carotene, while green vegetables are thought to help regulate metabolism.

Serves 2

1 clove garlic, peeled and finely minced

½ teaspoon salt

1 tablespoon finely chopped fresh cilantro

½ pound medium shrimp, peeled and deveined, tails removed

2 tablespoons extra-virgin olive oil

½ medium green bell pepper, seeded and thinly sliced

½ medium red bell pepper, seeded and thinly sliced

1 Combine garlic, salt, cilantro, and shrimp in a small bowl. Set aside.

2 Add the oil to the rice cooker, cover, and set to Cook. When the base of the pot gets warm, add the seasoned shrimp and cook about 7 minutes until shrimp turn pink.

3 Add the bell peppers and cook for 6 minutes or until peppers become tender and shrimp completely cook through. Serve immediately.

Creamed Corn Crabcakes

The tried-and-true pairing of corn and crab has always been available in chowders, but just wait until you try it in crabcake form. The crispy edges of the patties are met with each creamy and decadent mouthful.

Serves 3

3 green onions
12 ounces lump crabmeat, drained and shells removed
½ cup creamed corn
⅔ cup panko bread crumbs
½ teaspoon prepared horseradish
½ teaspoon salt
½ teaspoon ground black pepper
⅛ teaspoon ground nutmeg
⅛ teaspoon cayenne pepper
2 tablespoons olive oil

1 Slice green onions, separating whites and greens.

2 In a medium bowl, combine green onion whites, crabmeat, creamed corn, bread crumbs, horseradish, salt, black pepper, nutmeg, and cayenne. Form mixture into 6 patties.

3 Add 1 tablespoon oil to the rice cooker, cover, and set to Cook. When the base of the pot gets warm, cook 3 of the crabcakes for 3 minutes per side covered until browned and cooked through. Remove crabcakes and repeat with remaining oil and the other 3 crabcakes.

4 Garnish crabcakes with green onion greens.

Salmon and Asparagus en Papillote

Cooking a meal "en papillote" is simply a way of cooking with parchment paper packets. There are plenty of online tutorials demonstrating the process, and parchment cooking bags are available in most grocery stores. Serve each packet on a plate to your guests and they'll feel as if they are receiving a little gift for dinner!

Serves 2

- 2 (5-ounce) salmon fillets, about 1 inch thick
- 2 teaspoons chopped fresh dill
- 2 teaspoons salt
- 2 parchment-paper cooking bags
- 1 bunch asparagus, woody ends trimmed
- 4 teaspoons diced shallot
- 2 tablespoons butter, cut into 4 pats
- 4 slices lemon
- 2 cups water

1 Season salmon with dill and salt. Place each fillet in a parchment cooking bag. Place asparagus next to the fillet and evenly distribute shallot, butter, and lemon over top. Crimp edges together so that packets are sealed.

2 Pour water into rice cooker. Insert steamer basket. Place bags in steamer.

3 Set rice cooker to Cook. Cover and cook for about 7 minutes. Note that you won't be able to see the fish inside the packets. If your fillets are much thicker or thinner than 1 inch, adjust cooking time and open one packet to check for doneness. Remove packets from rice cooker and allow to rest for 5 minutes. Serve warm.

Quick Seafood Jambalaya

Let your rice cooker take you on a quick trip to New Orleans with this dish. Just be aware that "Creole seasoning" can mean many things—and many spice levels. Pick one with a heat index to your liking; any will work just fine in this recipe.

Serves 4

3 tablespoons butter

¼ cup diced onion

¼ cup diced red bell peppers

1 celery stalk, diced

3 cloves garlic, peeled and minced

1½ cups long-grain white rice

1 (15-ounce) can diced tomatoes, including juice

3 cups water

1 teaspoon salt

2 teaspoons Creole seasoning

½ pound sliced smoked sausage, fully cooked

½ pound medium shrimp, peeled and deveined

4 tablespoons chopped fresh parsley

1 Add butter to rice cooker and set to Cook. When the base of the cooker gets warm, add onion, bell peppers, and celery. Cook for 1 minute. Cover and cook for 3 minutes more until onions are translucent. Stir in garlic.

2 Add rice, tomatoes, water, salt, Creole seasoning, and sausage. Cover and cook for 20 minutes.

3 Stir in shrimp. Let simmer covered for 5 minutes on Warm setting.

4 Turn cooker off and let pot sit covered for 5 minutes. Ladle into bowls and serve warm. Garnish with parsley.

Chicken Main Dishes

Chicken is the most common domesticated fowl in America, as well as one the more popular proteins. Chicken has the great ability to take on the flavors that you season it with, making it versatile to cook with throughout the week. From Chicken Lettuce Wraps and Mushroom-Swiss Chicken Hoagies to Chicken Parm Meatballs and Chicken Fajitas, the dishes in this chapter will be perfectly steamed without drying out the meat, and you'll have minimal cleanup!

Chicken Barley Stew

It's okay if your taste buds don't exactly light up at the mention of the word "barley," but this often-overlooked grass is worth a new look. Barley provides a subtle, light-but-savory quality that can't be duplicated.

Serves 2

4 cups water

2 ounces washed and cleaned pearl barley, soaked for 4 hours before using

2 tablespoons vegetable oil

1 medium shallot, peeled and thinly sliced

1 clove garlic, peeled and finely minced

½ teaspoon grated ginger

1 boneless chicken thigh, sliced into bite-sized pieces

6 fresh shiitake mushroom caps, thinly sliced

1 cup canned corn kernels, drained

¼ teaspoon ground black pepper

1 tablespoon finely chopped fresh cilantro, for garnish

1 Add the water, set the cooker to Cook, and bring the water to a boil. Once boiling, add the presoaked barley, cover, and boil for 20 minutes until barley softens. Reserving the barley liquid separately for later use, strain the barley and set aside.

2 Clean out the rice cooker and wipe dry. Add the oil, cover, and set to Cook. When the base of the pot gets warm, add the shallots and cook until soft, about 3 minutes. Add the garlic and ginger and cook for about 3 minutes until fragrant.

3 Add the chicken and cook for 3 minutes or until chicken browns, covered and stirring occasionally while cooking.

4 Add the barley and 2 cups reserved barley liquid. Cover and allow to come to a simmer.

5 Add the mushrooms, corn, salt, and pepper. Cover the rice cooker and allow to return to a simmer. When bubbling vigorously, uncover and stir for 2 minutes, then switch to Warm. Cover rice cooker and continue to cook for 10–15 minutes until chicken cooks through. Garnish with cilantro.

Cider Chicken Stew

Do you know your potatoes? In this or any other recipe that doesn't specify a variety, Yukon gold potatoes are almost always a great choice. Their medium starchiness gives them a forgiving consistency and a full flavor.

Serves 4

2 tablespoons vegetable oil

1 medium onion, peeled and sliced

4 chicken drumsticks, or 2 chicken legs

2 cups baby carrots

1 large potato, cubed

1 teaspoon corn flour

3 cups spiced apple cider

1 cup water, or more as needed

½ teaspoon ground white pepper

½ teaspoon ground black pepper

¼ teaspoon salt

1 Add the oil to the rice cooker, cover, and set to Cook. When the base of the pot gets warm, add onions and cook for about 5 minutes until soft.

2 Add chicken, carrots, and potatoes and cook for 2–3 minutes until chicken browns, covered and stirring occasionally while cooking. Sprinkle the corn flour over this mixture and mix well.

3 Add the cider, water, white pepper, and black pepper to the 4-cup mark on the rice cooker or enough to immerse the chicken. Cover rice cooker and allow to come to a boil.

4 Switch the cooker to Warm, add the salt, cover rice cooker, and simmer until chicken cooks through, about 1 hour.

Caprese Chicken

All the Mediterranean flavors of an Italian caprese salad are here, but this is a chicken dish—and a truly delicious and simple one at that. Simpler still: while fresh is preferred, you can substitute any mozzarella.

Serves 4

- 3 (½-pound) skinless, boneless chicken breasts, quartered
- 1 (15-ounce) can diced tomatoes, with juice
- ¼ cup Chicken Stock (see Chapter 2)
- 2 tablespoons balsamic vinegar
- 1 tablespoon Italian seasoning
- 1 teaspoon salt
- ½ teaspoon ground black pepper
- 1 (8-ounce) ball sliced fresh mozzarella
- 1 tablespoon olive oil
- ¼ cup fresh basil leaves
- 1 loaf crusty bread, cut into ¼-inch pieces

1. Add the chicken, tomatoes, stock, vinegar, Italian seasoning, and salt and pepper to rice cooker; cover and set to Cook. Cook for 15 minutes.

2. Add the mozzarella to the top of the chicken. Switch cooker to Warm and heat for an additional 4 minutes or until cheese is melted.

3. Using a slotted spoon, transfer chicken and tomatoes to a serving dish. Drizzle with the olive oil. Garnish with the basil and serve warm with bread pieces.

Chicken in Wine and Shallot Sauce

The use of wine in cooking accentuates the flavors and aroma of food and should never overpower. Dry white wine is recommended when cooking savory dishes like this one—pinot grigio and sauvignon blanc are two of the best.

Serves 2

3 tablespoons extra-virgin olive oil

4 medium shallots, peeled and thinly sliced

2 (½-pound) skinless, boneless chicken breasts

1 teaspoon Worcestershire sauce

½ cup Chicken Stock (see Chapter 2)

2 tablespoons dry white wine, divided

2 tablespoons lemon juice

1 teaspoon chopped fresh parsley

1. Add the oil to the rice cooker, cover, and set to Cook. When the base of the pot gets warm, add shallots and cook about 3 minutes until slightly soft.

2. Add the chicken and cook each side about 5 minutes until brown, covering intermittently.

3. Add the Worcestershire sauce, stock, and 1 tablespoon wine. Mix well, cover rice cooker, and allow it to come to a simmer. Once simmering, switch to Warm and continue to simmer for about 10 minutes until chicken cooks through.

4. Stir in lemon juice and parsley. Sprinkle in remaining wine. Serve warm.

Pesto Chicken and Potatoes

Even from a jar, pesto bursts with fresh flavors, and its oil and herbs make any dish flavorful. This classic Mediterranean dish is a great choice when you have just a few ingredients in your refrigerator and need a great meal on short notice.

Serves 2

2 (½-pound) skinless, boneless chicken breasts, quartered

½ cup pesto

2 large russet potatoes, peeled and cut into 1-inch cubes

2 tablespoons butter

1 teaspoon salt

2 cups water

1 In a medium bowl, toss the pesto and chicken. Set aside.

2 Add the potatoes, butter, salt, and water to rice cooker, cover, and set to Cook. When the base of the cooker gets warm, let cook for 5 minutes.

3 Layer the chicken and pesto on top of the potatoes. Cover and cook for an additional 15 minutes until chicken is no longer pink in the center.

4 Transfer the chicken and the potatoes to bowls and serve warm.

Creamy Mushroom Chicken

A great last-minute meal, this savory dish is packed with veggies and couldn't be easier to make, and in a pinch you can even buy the mushrooms and broccoli sliced. Get this to the table on those tough, busy nights without sacrificing flavor or nutrients.

Serves 4

2 pounds boneless chicken breasts, cut into 1-inch cubes

1 (10¾-ounce) can condensed cream of mushroom soup

2 cups fresh sliced button mushrooms

2 cups chopped broccoli

1 cup water

½ cup whole milk

1 tablespoon Italian seasoning

1 teaspoon ground black pepper

1 Add all ingredients to rice cooker, cover, and set to Cook.

2 Cook for 10 minutes. Switch to Warm and simmer for an additional 5 minutes. Transfer to dishes and serve warm.

Chicken Fajitas

What a great meal to fix family-style so everyone can make fajitas to their liking. Note that while these are not listed among the ingredients, fajitas are always best served complete with a serve-yourself suite of condiments: sour cream, guacamole, salsa, shredded lettuce, sliced limes, jalapeños, shredded cheese, or whatever suits your table.

Serves 10

2 pounds skinless, boneless chicken breasts, sliced into ½-inch strips

1 small green bell pepper, seeded and sliced

1 small red bell pepper, seeded and sliced

1 small yellow bell pepper, seeded and sliced

1 small sweet onion, peeled and sliced

1 tablespoon olive oil

1 teaspoon salt

½ teaspoon ground black pepper

1 tablespoon chili powder

1 tablespoon ground cumin

1 cup water

10 (8-inch) flour tortillas

1 In a medium bowl, add the chicken, bell peppers, onions, oil, salt, black pepper, chili powder, and cumin; toss to combine. Cover and chill in the refrigerator for at least 20 minutes.

2 Cover the rice cooker and set to Cook. When the base of the pot gets warm, add the chicken mixture. Cook for 2 minutes until onions start to become tender. Add the water. Cover and cook for 7 minutes.

3 Uncover and stir. Switch cooker to Warm and cook for an additional 3 minutes.

4 Using a slotted spoon, transfer to a serving bowl. Serve warm with the tortillas.

Chicken Lettuce Wraps

These fresh lettuce wraps are perfect for a light dinner or, even better, for an afternoon lunch outdoors, maybe even with a little pinot grigio on the side. Both crunchy and tender, spicy and sweet, this dish hits the midday spot.

Serves 4

- 2 pounds ground chicken
- 1 cup finely diced shiitake mushrooms
- ½ cup chopped green onions
- ½ cup diced red bell pepper
- 5 cloves garlic, peeled and minced
- 2 tablespoons minced fresh ginger
- 2 tablespoons sesame oil
- ½ cup slivered almonds
- ½ cup reduced-sodium soy sauce
- 2 tablespoons rice vinegar
- 2 tablespoons sriracha
- 2 tablespoons honey
- ½ teaspoon salt
- ½ teaspoon ground white pepper
- ½ cup water
- 10–12 iceberg lettuce leaves

1 In a large bowl, combine all ingredients except for the water and lettuce leaves. Cover the rice cooker and set to Cook. When the base of the pot gets warm, add chicken mixture. Cook covered for 2 minutes.

2 Uncover and stir. Cook covered for an additional minute. Uncover and stir. Add water. Cover and cook for 8 minutes.

3 Uncover and switch heat to Warm. Cook uncovered for 3 minutes, stirring once or twice.

4 Using a slotted spoon, transfer mixture to a serving dish. Serve warm with lettuce leaves and create wraps.

Tex-Mex Chicken

Talk with your cheesemonger about varieties of Mexican cheeses, such as queso fresco and queso añejo, that would also be nice crumbled on top of this chicken dish. And if you're not feeling especially adventurous, Cheddar is always good!

Serves 4

- 1½ pounds skinless, boneless chicken thighs
- 2 tablespoons taco seasoning
- 1 tablespoon olive oil
- ¼ cup diced onion
- ¼ cup diced green bell pepper
- 1 (15¼-ounce) can sweet corn, drained
- 1 (15-ounce) can black beans, drained and rinsed
- 1 (4½-ounce) can chopped green chilies
- 1 (2¼-ounce) can sliced black olives, drained
- 1 can diced tomatoes, with juice
- ½ cup chopped fresh cilantro, divided
- 1 cup shredded manchego cheese

1. Season the chicken thighs with taco seasoning. Set aside.

2. Add the oil to the cooker and set to Cook. When the base of the pot gets warm, add the onion and the bell pepper. Stir-fry for 3 minutes until onions are translucent.

3. Add the chicken and toss. Add the corn, black beans, chilies, olives, tomatoes and juice, and ¼ cup cilantro. Cover and cook for about 10 minutes. Switch to Warm and heat for an additional 5 minutes until chicken is cooked through.

4. Transfer pot ingredients to a serving bowl. Serve warm and garnish with remaining cilantro and manchego cheese.

Chicken Bites with Green Olives

The bright, briny juices in a jar of green olives make a perfect marinade base for these savory little chicken bites. You can also try this with kalamata olive brine and garnish with feta cheese for some Greek flair!

Serves 4

1 tablespoon tomato paste
¼ cup green olive juice
1 tablespoon yellow mustard
1 teaspoon Italian seasoning
½ teaspoon garlic powder
Pinch cayenne pepper
1 teaspoon honey
2 tablespoons olive oil
1 teaspoon salt
1½ pounds skinless, boneless chicken thighs, cut into 1-inch cubes
½ cup halved green olives
1 cup water
2 tablespoons all-purpose flour
2 tablespoons fresh thyme leaves

1 In a medium bowl, whisk together the tomato paste, olive juice, mustard, Italian seasoning, garlic powder, cayenne, honey, olive oil, and salt. Toss in the chicken. Refrigerate covered for at least 30 minutes and up to 2 hours.

2 Switch rice cooker to Cook. When the base of the pot gets warm, add the chicken and the marinade. Stir in olives and water. Cover and cook for 10 minutes.

3 Uncover, switch to Warm, and cook for 3 minutes. Using a slotted spoon, transfer the chicken and olives to a serving dish.

4 Whisk the flour into the liquid remaining in the cooker and continue whisking for about 2 minutes on Warm until a sauce forms and thickens. Ladle over chicken. Garnish with thyme.

Orange-Maple Chicken Legs

These citrusy, sticky legs are perfect eaten straight from the rice cooker, but if you like your chicken on the crispy side, place these legs under the broiler before serving for about 3 and no more than 5 minutes or you'll risk burning.

Serves 4

1 medium orange
½ cup pure maple syrup
1 tablespoon soy sauce
1 teaspoon sriracha
¼ teaspoon ground ginger
1 teaspoon salt
2 pounds chicken legs
1 cup water
2 tablespoons fresh parsley
   leaves

1 Zest the orange until you have 2 teaspoons. Cut orange in half and juice. Slice orange halves into thin slices and set aside.

2 In a medium bowl, add the zest, orange juice, maple syrup, soy sauce, sriracha, ginger, and salt and stir to combine. Add chicken and refrigerate for 30 minutes.

3 Add the chicken, sauce, and water to rice cooker. Place the orange quarters around the chicken in the cooker.

4 Cover and set the rice cooker to Cook. After 20 minutes, switch cooker to Warm and simmer for an additional 5 minutes until legs are cooked through. Transfer the legs to a plate, top with parsley, and serve warm.

Mushroom-Swiss Chicken Hoagies

Mushroom and Swiss is a classic combination, but the addition of juicy chicken breast takes this hoagie to the next level. The peppery flavor of the arugula enhances the flavors alongside the horseradish mustard. If the spice from the horseradish seems like too much, use yellow mustard instead.

Serves 4

- 3 (½-pound) skinless, boneless chicken breasts, sliced into ½-inch strips
- 1 teaspoon salt
- 1 teaspoon ground black pepper
- 1 tablespoon olive oil
- 1 small sweet onion, peeled and thinly sliced
- 2 cups sliced button mushrooms
- 1 cup water
- 4 hoagie or sub rolls
- 4 tablespoons mayonnaise
- 4 tablespoons horseradish mustard
- 8 slices Swiss cheese
- 4 small handfuls arugula

1 Season the chicken with the salt and pepper. Set aside.

2 Add the oil to rice cooker, cover, and set to Cook. When the base of the pot gets warm, add the chicken strips and onion. Stir-fry for 1–2 minutes until the onions are translucent. Add the mushrooms and water. Cover and cook for 7 minutes.

3 Uncover. Switch cooker to Warm and heat for an additional 3 minutes. Using a slotted spoon, transfer the chicken and vegetables to a plate.

4 Prepare the hoagie rolls by spreading mayonnaise on one bun and mustard on the other. Distribute the chicken and veggies evenly among the buns. Add the Swiss cheese and arugula. Serve warm.

Chicken Parm Meatballs

Ground chicken has a tendency to dry out when cooked, but not in your rice cooker, and not with the addition of the sour cream. The onions and carrots add moisture, making sure these little meatballs are juicy and tasty!

Serves 4

¼ cup sour cream

¼ cup panko bread crumbs

1 tablespoon whole milk

1 pound ground chicken

2 tablespoons peeled and finely diced onion

1 small carrot, peeled and grated

1 large egg

4 tablespoons grated Parmesan cheese, divided

1 tablespoon Italian seasoning

½ teaspoon salt

½ teaspoon ground black pepper

2 tablespoons olive oil, divided

2 cups marinara sauce

½ cup water

¼ cup julienned fresh basil

1 In a medium bowl, add the sour cream, bread crumbs, and milk and stir to combine. Using your hands, massage in chicken, onion, carrot, egg, 2 tablespoons Parmesan, Italian seasoning, salt, and pepper. Form into 24 meatballs.

2 Add 1 tablespoon of the oil to the rice cooker, cover, and set to Cook. When the base of the pot gets warm, cook 12 meatballs on all sides for 3–4 minutes. Transfer to a plate. Repeat cooking with remaining oil and meatballs.

3 Add all meatballs to the pot. Add the marinara sauce and water. Cover and cook for 10 minutes.

4 Transfer meatballs and sauce to a serving dish and garnish with the remaining 2 tablespoons Parmesan and the basil.

Pork Main Dishes

Worldwide, pork is the most consumed protein. And is there any question as to why? Well, bacon for one, whether you are consuming the back or the belly. And pork chops for another, bone-in or bone-out. Each of the many cuts are unique in their texture, flavor, and use. The saltiness and almost sweetness of this savory meat can't be matched. Its unique flavor and fattiness lends itself to tender cuts, giving home chefs a leg up before almost any recipe is even started. The trapped steam from the rice cooker does a phenomenal job creating tender cuts of pork. From Cubano Pork Chops and Adobo Glazed Boneless Pork Chops to Pork Tenderloin with Cherry-Sage Sauce to Country-Style Pork Ribs with Baked Beans, this chapter is not short on taste or options.

Ground Pork with Mushrooms

The flavors of this dish are luscious right out of the cooker and become even more intense in the refrigerator overnight. It makes a complete meal served over white rice. Make a little extra by doubling this recipe and enjoy leftovers for lunch.

Serves 4

2 tablespoons soy sauce

1 tablespoon oyster sauce

½ tablespoon brown sugar

3 tablespoons warm water

1 tablespoon vegetable oil

1 pound ground pork

4 medium shallots, peeled and thinly sliced

2 cloves garlic, peeled and finely minced

6 fresh shiitake mushroom caps, finely diced

3 cups water, divided

¼ teaspoon salt

¼ teaspoon ground white pepper

1   In a small bowl, add soy sauce, oyster sauce, brown sugar, and warm water and mix. Set aside as sauce.

2   Add the oil to the rice cooker, cover, and set to Cook. When the base of the pot gets warm, add the pork, breaking into smaller bits with a spatula, and cook about 10 minutes or until pork browns. Leaving the remaining oil in the pot, dish out the partially cooked pork and set aside.

3   Add the shallots to the pot and cook about 3 minutes until soft. Add the garlic and mushrooms and cook about 3 minutes more or until fragrant.

4   Add 1 cup of the water and the salt and pepper. Cover and allow the mixture to reach a simmer.

5   Return the pork to the pot. Add the sauce and 2 cups water or enough to immerse the entire mixture. Stir well, cover, and simmer for about 20 minutes, stirring occasionally. Switch to Warm if mixture bubbles too vigorously. Switch to Warm before serving.

Cubano Pork Chops

Everything great that you find on the classic Cubano sandwich is brought to life in this one-pot dish. Don't skip those pickle slices as they add that special something to this dish. Serve on artisanal crusty bread for the full effect.

Serves 2

2 (¾-pound) boneless pork chops, about 1 inch thick

2 tablespoons yellow mustard

1 tablespoon olive oil

2 cups water

4 thin ham slices (sandwich meat)

8 dill pickle slices

4 slices Swiss cheese

1 Slather all sides of pork chops with mustard. Set aside.

2 Add oil to rice cooker and set to Cook. When the base of the cooker gets warm, add pork chops. Sear until browned, about 3 minutes per side. Remove from cooker and place in a steamer basket.

3 Pour water into rice cooker. Add steamer basket with pork chops. Cover and cook for 14 minutes. Add ham slices and dill pickle slices atop pork chops. Cover with Swiss cheese. Switch heat to Warm and simmer covered for 2 minutes. Serve warm.

Pork with Potatoes, Peas, and Corn

Unlike the Ground Pork with Mushrooms (see recipe in this chapter), in which you could scale up on the quantity and cook more, the vegetables in this dish tend to turn mushy when reheated. Therefore, it is recommended that you cook only enough for just one meal. Serve with white rice for a complete meal.

Serves 2

1 tablespoon soy sauce
1 teaspoon oyster sauce
1 teaspoon brown sugar
3 tablespoons warm water
3 tablespoons vegetable oil
½ pound ground pork
2 medium shallots, peeled and thinly sliced
1 clove garlic, peeled and finely minced
1 medium potato, peeled and cut into ½-inch cubes
½ cup frozen peas (or canned)
½ cup frozen corn (or canned)
3 cups water, divided
¼ teaspoon salt
¼ teaspoon ground white pepper

1   In a small bowl, add soy sauce, oyster sauce, brown sugar, and warm water and mix. Set aside as sauce.

2   Add the oil to the rice cooker, cover, and set to Cook. When the base of the pot gets warm, add ground pork, break into small bits, and cook until browned, about 10 minutes. Dish out the partially cooked pork and set aside. Leave the remaining oil in the pot.

3   Add the shallots and cook about 3 minutes until soft. Add the garlic, potatoes, peas, and corn and cook about 5 minutes until aromatic, covered and stirring occasionally while cooking.

4   Add 1 cup water, salt, and pepper. Cover rice cooker and allow the mixture to reach a simmer.

5   Once simmering, return the partially cooked pork to the pot. Add the sauce and 2 cups water or enough to partially immerse the entire mixture. Stir well, cover the rice cooker, and allow the pork to cook in the simmering mixture for about 20 minutes, switching to Warm if mixture bubbles too vigorously. Keep at Warm before serving.

Pork in Tomato Sauce

Ketchup gives a sweet-and-sour aspect to this appetizing pork dish. It can be served with rice and is perfect as a sandwich filler too.

Serves 2

1 (½-pound) pork tenderloin, thinly sliced
1 teaspoon soy sauce
¼ teaspoon salt
¼ teaspoon ground white pepper
½ teaspoon honey
1 tablespoon ketchup
½ cup water
1 teaspoon corn flour
3 tablespoons vegetable oil

1   In a medium bowl, add the pork, soy sauce, salt, pepper, and honey and stir to combine. Place in the refrigerator and marinate for 30 minutes.

2   In a separate small bowl, add ketchup, water, and corn flour and combine. Set aside as sauce.

3   Add the oil to the rice cooker, cover, and set to Cook. When the base of the pot gets warm, add the pork and cook about 8–10 minutes until browned and partially cooked through. Remove from pot and set aside. Leave the remaining oil in the pot.

4   Add the prepared sauce to the pot, stir well, cover rice cooker, and allow to reach a simmer. Once simmering, return the pork to the pot, cover, and let it simmer for about 8–10 minutes. If mixture bubbles too vigorously, switch to Warm and continue to simmer until the pork cooks through and sauce reduces (thickens).

Pork Chops with Apple-Cabbage Slaw

The heartiness of the pork chops is complemented by the light and crunchy nature of the fresh slaw. If you have some jicama lying around or have been curious to try it, you can substitute it for the apples.

Serves 2

Slaw
2 cups shredded red cabbage

1 cup peeled and grated carrots

1 medium Granny Smith apple, peeled, cored, and julienned

2 medium shallots, peeled and minced

1 teaspoon orange zest

1 tablespoon freshly squeezed orange juice

1 tablespoon olive oil

1 tablespoon apple cider vinegar

½ teaspoon sea salt

2 teaspoons honey

1 teaspoon sriracha

¼ cup chopped fresh parsley

Pork Chops
2 (¾-pound) boneless pork chops, about 1 inch thick

1 teaspoon salt

½ teaspoon ground black pepper

1 tablespoon olive oil

2 cups water

2 tablespoons fresh parsley leaves

1 **For the Slaw:** Combine slaw ingredients in a medium bowl. Refrigerate covered for 30 minutes up to overnight. Taste before serving. Add more salt if necessary.

2 **For the Pork Chops:** Season pork chops on both sides with salt and pepper.

3 Add oil to rice cooker and set to Cook. When the base of the cooker gets warm, add pork chops. Sear until browned, about 3 minutes per side. Remove from cooker and place in a steamer basket.

4 Place water in pot. Insert steamer basket and place lid on cooker. Heat for 14 minutes. Transfer pork chops to a serving plate and let rest for 5 minutes. Top with slaw and garnish with parsley leaves. Serve warm.

Hawaiian-Style BBQ Pork Meatballs

These sweet and tangy meatballs are perfect on their own; however, try them over rice or pasta or even in lettuce wraps or on submarine rolls. Any way you roll it, they rock!

Serves 4

¾ cup Heinz Hawaii Style BBQ Sauce

¼ cup water

1 (8-ounce) can crushed pineapple, 2 tablespoons reserved

1 pound ground pork

1 large whisked egg

⅔ cup bread crumbs

2 tablespoons finely diced red onion

¼ teaspoon seeded and finely diced habanero pepper

1 tablespoon dried cilantro

¼ teaspoon salt

⅛ teaspoon ground cinnamon

2 tablespoons olive oil

1 In a medium bowl, add BBQ sauce, water, and all but 2 tablespoons of the crushed pineapple and stir to combine. Set aside.

2 In a large bowl, add 2 tablespoons crushed pineapple, pork, egg, bread crumbs, red onion, habanero pepper, cilantro, salt, and cinnamon and stir to combine. Form into 24 meatballs.

3 Add oil to the rice cooker, cover, and set to Cook. When the base of the pot gets warm, add meatballs. Cover and cook for 2 minutes. Uncover and roll meatballs for 3 minutes until they are seared and no longer pink on the outside.

4 Add BBQ mixture to pot. Toss to cover meatballs. Cover and cook for 10 minutes. Transfer meatballs and sauce to a serving platter.

Adobo Glazed Boneless Pork Chops

Adobo sauce can be found in most grocery stores in the ethnic or Hispanic aisle. It is a glorious smoky and spicy sauce that adds depth to sauces, chilies, and meats. Use sparingly and taste as you go while making the sauce to adjust to your heat level.

Serves 2

- 4 teaspoons balsamic vinegar
- 4 tablespoons honey
- 2 tablespoons adobo sauce
- 2 (¾-pound) boneless pork chops, about 1 inch thick
- 1 teaspoon salt
- ½ teaspoon ground black pepper
- 1 tablespoon olive oil
- 2 cups water
- 2 cloves garlic, peeled and quartered

1 In a small bowl, add balsamic vinegar, honey, and adobo sauce and stir to combine. Refrigerate until needed.

2 Season pork chops on both sides with salt and pepper.

3 Add oil to rice cooker and set to Cook. When the base of the cooker gets warm, add pork chops. Sear until browned, about 3 minutes per side. Remove from cooker. Brush ⅓ of the sauce on the pork chops and place in a steamer basket.

4 Place water and garlic cloves in pot. Insert steamer basket and place lid on cooker. Cook for 7 minutes. Brush another ⅓ of the sauce on the pork chops and cook for another 7 minutes. Transfer pork chops to a serving plate and brush with remaining sauce. Let rest for 5 minutes. Serve warm.

Quick-Breaded Herbed Pork Chops

This quick summery meal always yields juicy pork chops when prepared with a rice cooker, from the cookers steaming abilities and also from the mayonnaise, which adds a layer of moistness that helps both hold the herbs and bread crumbs together and seal the juices in.

Serves 2

- ¼ cup panko bread crumbs
- 1 tablespoon Italian seasoning
- 1 teaspoon salt
- 2 tablespoons mayonnaise
- 2 (¾-pound) bone-in pork chops, 1 inch thick
- 2 tablespoons olive oil
- 2 cups water

1. In a small bowl, mix together the bread crumbs, Italian seasoning, and salt. Set aside.

2. Rub mayonnaise over pork chops. Coat pork with bread crumb mixture. Set aside.

3. Add oil to rice cooker and set to Cook. When the base of the cooker gets warm, add pork chops. Sear until browned, about 3 minutes per side. Remove pork chops and place in a steamer basket.

4. Add water to rice cooker. Insert steamer basket with pork chops. Cook lidded for 15 minutes.

5. Transfer pork chops to 2 plates. Serve warm.

Greek Pork Chops with Feta Cheese

These aren't your grandma's pork chops. This Mediterranean twist on the classic down-home pork chop dish will have you coming back for more, and because you're using your rice cooker, you don't have to worry about overcooking the meat.

Serves 2

2 (¾-pound) bone-in pork chops, 1 inch thick

1 tablespoon Italian seasoning

1 teaspoon salt

½ teaspoon ground black pepper

1 tablespoon olive oil

1 (14½-ounce can) diced tomatoes, with juice

½ cup halved kalamata olives, pitted

1 cup water

¼ cup feta cheese

2 tablespoons julienned fresh basil

1 Season pork chops on both sides with Italian seasoning, salt, and pepper.

2 Add oil to rice cooker and set to Cook. When the base of the cooker gets warm, add pork chops. Sear until browned, about 3 minutes per side. Add tomatoes and juice, olives, and water. Cook covered for 14 minutes.

3 Transfer pork chops, tomatoes, and olives to 2 plates. Garnish with feta cheese and fresh basil.

Pork Tenderloin with Cherry-Sage Sauce

The sage in this dish nods to the fall, but you can freshen it up for any season by substituting some freshly chopped parsley. Also, cherries pair beautifully with pork, so go ahead and try some other stone fruit jams and preserves such as apricot, peach, and plum to change up this new family favorite.

Serves 2

½ cup cherry preserves
½ cup freshly squeezed orange juice
2 tablespoons water
1 teaspoon ground sage
1 (1¼-pound) pork tenderloin
1 teaspoon salt
½ teaspoon ground black pepper
1 tablespoon olive oil

1 In a small bowl, add cherry preserves, orange juice, water, and sage and stir to combine. Set aside.

2 Place tenderloin on a cutting board and slice in half. Season all sides with salt and pepper.

3 Add oil to the rice cooker, cover, and set to Cook. When the base of the pot gets warm, add pork and sear for 2–3 minutes per side until browned.

4 Spoon cherry mixture over pork and add remaining liquid to the cooker. Cover and continue to cook until the rice cooker switches to Warm.

5 Transfer pork to a serving tray and spoon cherry liquid over the pork. Let rest for 5 minutes. Slice and serve.

Country-Style Pork Ribs with Baked Beans

You'll find this cut in the meat section at your grocery store. Pork loin boneless country-style ribs aren't actually ribs at all. Usually cut from the shoulder, they are not only ideal for grilling, but they are good for low-and-slow cooking due to the beautiful marbling they have.

Serves 4

- 1½ pounds pork loin boneless country-style ribs
- 1 tablespoon olive oil
- 1 tablespoon salt
- 1 teaspoon ground white pepper
- 1 teaspoon Italian seasoning
- 1 teaspoon ground cumin
- 1 teaspoon ground mustard
- 1 medium onion, peeled and roughly chopped
- 4 cups water
- 1 (16-ounce) can baked beans, with juice

1. In a large bowl, add pork and olive oil and toss to combine. Set aside.

2. In a small bowl, whisk together salt, pepper, Italian seasoning, cumin, and mustard. Sprinkle over pork and massage into meat using your hands. Refrigerate for 30 minutes.

3. Add meat to rice cooker. Scatter chopped onions around meat. Add water. Cover.

4. Set rice cooker to Cook. When the water starts to boil, let cook for 15 minutes. Switch heat to Warm. Allow to simmer for about 1 hour.

5. Uncover. Discard 3 cups of cooking liquid. Add baked beans including juice. Let simmer for an additional 5 minutes.

6. Transfer the pork, beans, and onions to a serving platter. Let rest for 5 minutes. Pour a spoonful or two of liquid from rice cooker over pork. Serve warm.

Pecan-Crusted Boneless Pork with Honey Mustard Sauce

This fresh take on pork chops is great for kids or the fussy eaters in your house, thanks especially to the the very recognizable and popular honey mustard sauce. Substitute different kinds of mustard for some flair and a change of flavor, or serve more than one variety on the side and let your diners choose for themselves!

Serves 2

Honey Mustard Sauce
¼ cup mayonnaise
¼ cup honey
¼ cup yellow mustard
1 tablespoon apple cider vinegar
⅛ teaspoon cayenne pepper
Dash of Worcestershire sauce

Pork
2 (¾-pound) boneless pork chops, about 1 inch thick
1 teaspoon salt
1 tablespoon olive oil
4 tablespoons finely chopped pecans
2 cups water

1. **For the Honey Mustard Sauce:** Whisk together Honey Mustard Sauce ingredients in a small bowl. Refrigerate until ready to use.

2. **For the Pork:** Season pork chops with salt. Set aside.

3. Add oil to rice cooker and set to Cook. When the base of the cooker gets warm, add pork chops. Sear until browned, about 3 minutes per side. Remove from cooker. Brush ⅓ of the Honey Mustard Sauce on the pork chops and place in a steamer basket. Press pecans into the top of the pork chops.

4. Add water to rice cooker. Insert steamer basket with pork chops and place lid on cooker. Set to Cook and cook for 14 minutes. Transfer chops to 2 plates and serve with remaining Honey Mustard Sauce on the side.

Drunken Apple and Onion Pork Tenderloin

Depending on the type of beer you choose, this recipe can go any number of ways. It is probably best not to choose a stout, but otherwise it's hard to go wrong—from light beer to rich ales, just about anything turns out a wonderful dish. If you're avoiding alcohol or in a pinch, you can substitute chicken stock.

Serves 2

- 1 (1½-pound) pork tenderloin
- 2 tablespoons Dijon mustard
- 1 tablespoon olive oil
- 1 large onion, peeled, halved, and sliced
- 2 medium Granny Smith apples, cored and diced
- 2 teaspoons dried thyme
- 12 ounces beer
- 1 cup water

1 Place the tenderloin on a cutting board and slice in half. Brush all sides of the pork with mustard.

2 Add the oil to the rice cooker, cover, and set to Cook. When the base of the pot gets warm, add pork and sear for 2 minutes per side or until browned. Scatter the onion and apples in rice cooker. Add the thyme, beer, and water.

3 Cover and cook for 7 minutes. Switch to Warm and cook uncovered for an additional 5 minutes to allow some of the alcohol to cook off. Unplug the rice cooker.

4 Transfer the pork to a serving plate. Using a slotted spoon, transfer the onion and apples to the plate. Let the pork rest for 5 minutes. Slice and serve warm with the onion and apples.

Beef Main Dishes

Beef is about as American as you can get. And it's an extremely versatile protein to work with. Whether you're cooking roasts, ribs, or numerous cuts of steak, each lends a different delicious flavor and texture. The organs, or offal, are utilized for many delicacies, and their blood can be used in blood sausage for German dishes. Even the bones can be cooked to create a beautiful nutritional beef bone stock. And guess what? Your rice cooker will be your sous chef helping achieve beef perfection by stewing, braising, and steaming. From Mini Balsamic Meatloaves to Taco Tuesday Meatballs and Mojo Beef and Potatoes to Traditional Chuck Roast, the recipes in this chapter will take you around the world of spices and flavors.

Mini Beef Burger

For a less fatty version, use leaner meat. However, remember that lean meat will have less flavor and tends to dry out because it has less fat. That's why lean patties will usually be less tender, less moist, and less juicy when cooked. Or go with a 15–20 percent fat beef for a fuller flavor.

Serves 4

- 1 pound ground beef
- ½ medium, onion, peeled and grated
- 1 teaspoon minced garlic
- ½ teaspoon grated ginger
- 1 teaspoon Worcestershire sauce
- 1 teaspoon dried basil
- ½ teaspoon salt
- ½ teaspoon ground black pepper
- 1 egg
- 4 tablespoons extra-virgin olive oil, divided
- 4 burger buns, halved
- 4 slices mozzarella cheese
- 2 medium tomatoes, sliced and divided
- 10 lettuce leaves
- ½ medium onion, peeled and thinly sliced

1 Place the beef, grated onion, garlic, ginger, Worcestershire sauce, basil, salt, pepper, and egg in a large bowl. Mix with your hands until evenly combined. Divide into 4 burger patties, each about 3 inches in diameter and ½ inch thick.

2 Add 2 tablespoons oil to the rice cooker, cover, and set to Cook. When the base of the pot gets warm, add 2 patties and cook about 5 minutes on each side or until browned and cooked through. Cover rice cooker while cooking. Transfer the cooked patties to a plate, set aside, and cover with foil to keep warm. Repeat with the remaining oil and patties.

3 Place a patty on each burger bun and add cheese, tomatoes, lettuce, and sliced onions.

Beef Stew

This is a simple beef stew, meant to serve as a starting point. Some find the balance just right, and some cooks like something a bit heartier. If you're in that second group, try adding a couple tablespoons of diced bacon.

Serves 2

1 pound cubed beef stew meat
1 tablespoon corn flour
½ teaspoon salt
2 tablespoons olive oil
1 medium onion, peeled and sliced
1 medium carrot, peeled and sliced
2 celery stalks, sliced
2 cups warm water, or more as needed

1 Place the beef, corn flour, and salt in a large zip-top freezer bag. Shake to coat the beef with flour.

2 Add the oil to the rice cooker, cover, and set to Cook. When the base of the pot gets warm, add the beef and cook for 10 minutes until evenly browned. Leaving the remaining oil in the pot, remove the beef and set aside.

3 Add the onions and cook about 5 minutes until slightly soft, covered and stirring occasionally.

4 Return the beef to the pot. Add the carrots, celery, and enough warm water to partially cover the beef. Cover and allow mixture to reach a simmer.

5 Switch to Warm and continue to simmer for about 2 hours.

A Thickening Agent

The flour in this recipe not only seals the moisture in the beef, but it also helps to thicken the stew. Add about 1 cup peeled and cubed potatoes in step 4 for further thickening.

Mini Balsamic Meatloaves

These lend themselves well to a small-portion dinner that doesn't sacrifice gusto. Or go ahead and eat a whole plateful—they're miniature in size to allow for less cooking time and to allow steam from the rice cooker to deliver a moist, savory delight.

Serves 4

Balsamic Glaze

¼ cup ketchup
1 teaspoon yellow mustard
1 teaspoon balsamic vinegar

Mini Meatloaves

2 cups water
1 pound ground beef
2 tablespoons peeled and finely diced onion
¾ cups old-fashioned oats
1 large egg, whisked
½ cup ketchup
½ teaspoon Worcestershire sauce
½ teaspoon sriracha
½ teaspoon salt
½ teaspoon celery seed

1 **For the Balsamic Glaze:** Add the ketchup, mustard, and vinegar to a small bowl and stir to combine. Cover and refrigerate until needed.

2 **For the Mini Meatloaves:** Add the water to the pot; in a medium bowl, combine the remaining ingredients and stir to mix.

3 Form 4 meatloaves. Brush tops of loaves with ½ of the glaze and place in a steamer basket.

4 Insert the steamer basket into the rice cooker and cover. Set to cook for 10 minutes, then switch to Warm and cook for 10 minutes more.

5 Transfer the meatloaves to a plate and brush with the remaining glaze. Allow to rest for 10 minutes before serving.

Spicy Ground Beef

If you're ready to take your beef dishes to the next level, go out and find a meat grinder. You can start by buying chuck roast at the market and making your own grind at home. You'll be surprised how much of a difference you'll taste.

Serves 2

1 tablespoon vegetable oil
½ pound ground beef
1 tablespoon butter, divided
4 medium shallots, peeled and thinly sliced
1 clove garlic, peeled and finely minced
2 teaspoons grated ginger
1 fresh poblano pepper, seeded and sliced, divided
½ teaspoon chili powder
1 medium tomato, chopped
1 tablespoon finely chopped fresh cilantro, for garnish

1. Add the oil to the rice cooker, cover, and set to Cook. When the base of the pot gets warm, add the beef, break it into small bits using a spatula or cooking spoon, and cook for 10 minutes or until browned, covered and stirring occasionally. Leaving the remaining oil in the pot, remove the beef and set aside.

2. Add ½ tablespoon of the butter to the pot and allow to melt. Add the shallots and cook about 3 minutes until soft. Add the garlic and ginger and cook about 3 minutes until fragrant.

3. Add half of the sliced poblano, the chili powder, tomato, and remaining butter. Cook for 1 minute, covered and stirring occasionally.

4. Return the beef to the pot and cook covered until beef cooks through completely, about 10 minutes. Garnish with the cilantro and the remaining sliced poblano, then mix well.

Cilantro or Coriander?

The leaves of this herb are known as cilantro leaves, coriander leaves, or Chinese parsley in different parts of the world. The fruits are called coriander seeds. Both the leaves and the dried seeds are used in a wide range of cuisines.

Ground Beef with Peas

Peas are great in this dish, but if you fall in love with it—and you just might, because it's a great weeknight standby—you'll eventually want to mix things up a bit. Try broccoli, cutting the heads up into smaller florets to maintain the balance of each bite.

Serves 3

2 tablespoons vegetable oil
½ pound ground beef
2 cloves garlic, peeled and finely minced
½ tablespoon oyster sauce
1 cup water
¼ teaspoon ground black pepper
1 cup frozen peas
¼ teaspoon salt
¼ teaspoon ground white pepper
1 green onion, finely chopped, for garnish

1 Add the oil to the rice cooker, cover, and set to Cook. When the base of the pot gets warm, add the beef, break it into small bits using a spatula or cooking spoon, and cook for 10 minutes or until browned, covered and stirring occasionally. Leaving the remaining oil in the pot, remove the beef and set aside.

2 Add the garlic to the pot and cook about 3 minutes until fragrant. Add the oyster sauce, water, and the black pepper and stir well. Cover and allow mixture to come to a simmer.

3 Add the peas and return the beef to the pot, then add the salt and white pepper. Cover and allow mixture to cook until beef cooks through and peas become tender, about 10 minutes.

4 Switch to Warm a few minutes before serving. Garnish with the green onion.

Sloppy Joe-Loaded Potatoes

A sloppy joe is a different sandwich in different parts of the United States—this one isn't a sandwich at all! The classic family favorite gets an upgrade here when it's served inside a baked potato. Together, taste bud magic happens and folks will be asking for more.

Serves 4

- 4 large russet potatoes
- 3 tablespoons butter
- 3 green onions, sliced, whites and greens divided
- 1 small green bell pepper, seeded and finely diced
- 1 small carrot, peeled and finely diced
- 1 celery stalk, finely diced
- 1 pound ground beef
- 1 cup ketchup
- ½ cup water
- 1 tablespoon molasses
- 1 teaspoon chili powder
- 1 teaspoon ground mustard
- 1 teaspoon garlic powder
- ⅛ teaspoon cayenne pepper
- 4 tablespoons sour cream, for garnish
- ½ cup grated Cheddar cheese, for garnish

1 Preheat oven to 425°F. Prick the potatoes all over with a fork, then place on a baking sheet and bake for 50–60 minutes or until the flesh is soft and easily pierced with a knife.

2 Add the butter to rice cooker, cover, and set to Cook. When the base of the pot gets warm, add the green onions (reserving 1 tablespoon for garnish), bell pepper, carrot, celery, and ground beef. Break beef into smaller bits and cook covered for 2 minutes.

3 Uncover, stir, and cook covered for an additional minute. Uncover and cook for another 3 minutes or until beef is no longer pink.

4 Stir in the ketchup, water, molasses, chili powder, mustard, garlic powder, and cayenne. Cover and cook for 10 minutes. Uncover, stir, and switch heat to Warm. Cover pot and continue to cook for 10 minutes.

5 Cut a slit in the top of the baked potatoes and place in bowls. Squeeze potato on both ends to make a pocket. Ladle sloppy joe mixture over potatoes. Garnish with the sour cream, Cheddar cheese, and remaining 1 tablespoon green onion.

Cheeseburger Casserole

What a yummy twist on a drive-through classic. The pickle relish adds a little crunch and acidity to this dish that brings the scrumptious flavors of the beloved cheeseburger to a casserole. The noodles take on the task of the bun, and the tomato soup adds a creaminess that makes this dish irresistible. If you don't have parsley on hand, throw in a handful of shredded lettuce.

Serves 8

2 tablespoons butter

1 pound ground beef

1 small red onion, peeled and sliced

¼ cup dill pickle relish

2 tablespoons yellow mustard

1 teaspoon salt

1 (28-ounce) can diced tomatoes, with juice

1 (10¾-ounce) can condensed tomato soup

2 cups water

1 pound egg noodles

1 cup shredded Cheddar cheese

¼ cup chopped fresh parsley, for garnish

1 Add the butter to the rice cooker, cover, and set to Cook. When the base of the pot gets warm, add the beef and the onions. Break the beef into smaller bits, and cook covered for 2 minutes.

2 Uncover, stir, and cook for an additional minute. Uncover and stir-fry for another 3 minutes until the beef is no longer pink.

3 Add the relish, mustard, salt, diced tomatoes, tomato soup, water, and egg noodles. Stir to mix well. Cover and cook for 10 minutes. Stir again and switch heat to Warm. Cover and cook for 15 minutes.

4 Stir in the Cheddar cheese. Transfer to a serving dish. Garnish with the parsley and serve.

Swedish Meatballs with Egg Noodles

In no time at all you can serve up a traditional bowl of Swedish meatballs. You can make the meatballs the night before for quicker meal prep after a long day of work. Also, for you mushroom lovers, this is a great dish to add a cup of sliced mushrooms. Just toss them in with the noodles in step 3.

Serves 4

- ½ cup panko bread crumbs
- ¼ cup whole milk
- 1 pound ground beef
- ¼ cup finely diced red onion
- 1 large egg
- 3 teaspoons Worcestershire sauce, divided
- ¼ cup chopped fresh parsley
- 3 tablespoons butter
- 3 cups water
- 2 cups beef stock
- ½ pound egg noodles
- 1 cup sour cream
- 2 tablespoons all-purpose flour
- ½ teaspoon salt
- ¼ teaspoon ground white pepper
- 2 teaspoons Dijon mustard

1 In a medium bowl, add the bread crumbs and milk and stir to combine. Add the beef, onion, egg, 1 teaspoon Worcestershire sauce, and parsley and use your hands to mix to combine. Form into 24 meatballs.

2 Add the butter to the rice cooker, cover, and set to Cook. When the base of the pot gets warm, cook the meatballs on all sides until browned, about 4 minutes. Transfer to a plate and set aside.

3 Add the water, stock, and egg noodles to rice cooker. Place the meatballs on top of the noodles and cook for 10 minutes.

4 Remove 1½ cups of liquid from the rice cooker and switch heat to Warm. Stir in the sour cream, the remaining 2 teaspoons Worcestershire sauce, the flour, salt and pepper, and Dijon mustard. Cook about 4 minutes until the liquid thickens. Serve warm.

Mojo Beef and Potatoes

Although made in too many variations to count, mojo sauce is typically full of citrus and garlic flavors. Many Latin American countries put their traditional stamp on the sauce by mixing up the range of peppers, fruits, spices, and even colors of the sauce.

Serves 2

Mojo Sauce
¼ cup olive oil
½ cup orange marmalade
⅓ cup lime juice
⅓ cup lemon juice
1 tablespoon lime zest
1 tablespoon lemon zest
4 cloves garlic, peeled and minced
2 tablespoons maple syrup
2 teaspoons salt
2 teaspoons chili powder
¼ cup chopped fresh cilantro
¼ cup chopped fresh parsley

Beef and Potatoes
1 pound beef stew cubes
8 small red potatoes, halved
2 cups water

1 **For the Mojo Sauce:** In a medium bowl, whisk together all the Mojo Sauce ingredients. Toss beef into sauce. Refrigerate covered for 30 minutes.

2 **For the Beef and Potatoes:** Place potatoes in rice cooker. Add water, beef, and all of the Mojo Sauce. Cover and set to Cook. Once water starts to boil, heat for 5 minutes. Switch to Warm and simmer for an additional 10 minutes.

3 Transfer beef and potatoes to a serving dish.

Frito Pie

For a truly authentic Frito Pie experience, cut your bags of corn chips lengthwise, pour the chili and other condiments straight into the bags, and serve with a spoon. Your guests will thank you—as long as you provide plenty of napkins.

Serves 6

2 teaspoons olive oil

1 pound ground beef

1 (16-ounce) can chili beans or pinto beans in chili sauce, including sauce

1 (14½-ounce) can crushed tomatoes, with juice

1 (15-ounce) can corn, drained

1 teaspoon ground cumin

2 teaspoons chili powder

½ teaspoon salt

6 small bags Fritos or other corn chips

2 cups grated Cheddar cheese, for garnish

½ cup finely diced red onion, for garnish

1 Add the olive oil to rice cooker, cover, and set to Cook. When the base of the pot gets warm, add the beef, break it into smaller bits, and cook covered for 2 minutes.

2 Uncover, stir, and cook covered for an additional minute. Uncover and stir-fry for another 2–3 minutes until beef is no longer pink.

3 Stir in beans including sauce, tomatoes including juice, corn, cumin, chili powder, and salt. Cover and cook for 10 minutes. Uncover, stir, and switch heat to Warm. Cover pot and continue to cook on Warm for 10 minutes.

4 Serve chili warm atop corn chips. Garnish with Cheddar cheese and red onion.

Taco Tuesday Meatballs

A fresh take on Taco Tuesday, your family will ask for this recipe week after week. Serve this dish with saffron rice or with shredded lettuce, sour cream, cheese, black olives, and even fresh avocado slices to complete this tasty meal.

Serves 4

- ¼ cup panko bread crumbs
- ¼ cup whole milk
- 1 pound ground beef
- 2 tablespoons peeled and finely diced onion
- 2 tablespoons grated red bell pepper
- 1 large egg
- 2 tablespoons finely grated Cheddar cheese
- 1 tablespoon taco seasoning
- 1 teaspoon ground cumin
- 2 tablespoons olive oil, divided
- 1 (15-ounce) can diced tomatoes, including juice
- ½ cup water
- ¼ cup fresh cilantro, for garnish

1. In a medium bowl, combine the bread crumbs and milk and stir to mix. Add the beef, onion, bell pepper, egg, cheese, taco seasoning, and cumin and use your hands to mix to combine. Form into 24 meatballs.

2. Add 1 tablespoon of the oil to the rice cooker, cover, and set to Cook. When the base of the pot gets warm, cook 12 meatballs on all sides for 4 minutes. Transfer to a plate. Repeat cooking with remaining oil and meatballs. Add the plated meatballs to the pot with the freshly cooked ones. Add diced tomatoes and water. Cover and cook for 10 minutes.

3. Transfer the meatballs and sauce to a serving dish and garnish with cilantro.

Root Beer Beef Short Ribs

Ribs in a rice cooker? Yes! Root beer as flavoring? Oh yes! These ribs are so tender and tangy that you'll never cook them any other way. The garlic simply adds an aromatic while cooking. The sauce and rice cooker steam do the rest.

Serves 4

- 2½ pounds beef short ribs
- 1 teaspoon salt
- 1 teaspoon ground black pepper
- 2 tablespoons olive oil
- 6 cloves garlic, peeled and halved
- 2 tablespoons tomato paste
- 3 cups beef stock
- 20 ounces root beer

1 Season short ribs with salt and pepper. Set rice cooker to Cook and add olive oil. When the pot gets warm, add ribs. Cover and cook for 3 minutes. Flip ribs. Cover and cook for an additional 3 minutes.

2 Scatter garlic over ribs. Add tomato paste, stock, and root beer; stir to mix in paste. Cover.

3 Once liquid reaches a boil, cook for 10 minutes. Switch cooker to Warm and allow to simmer for 60 minutes. Transfer ribs to a platter and serve warm.

Traditional Chuck Roast

Don't worry about peeling your potatoes or carrots in this rustic dish. A lot of nutrients are found in those skins. Just make sure you give them a good scrubbing to remove any dirt these underground dwellers may have stuck to them.

Serves 4

- 1 (2-pound) chuck roast
- 1 teaspoon salt
- 2 teaspoons ground black pepper, divided
- 3 tablespoons butter
- 3 medium carrots, sliced into ½-inch pieces
- 2 celery stalks, sliced into ½-inch pieces
- 1 small onion, peeled and diced
- 1 small jalapeño, seeded and thinly sliced
- 2 small russet potatoes, diced
- 4 cups beef stock
- 1 tablespoon Worcestershire sauce
- 2 teaspoons garlic powder
- 2 tablespoons all-purpose flour

1 Season the chuck roast on all sides with salt and 1 teaspoon of the pepper. Set aside.

2 Set rice cooker to Cook and add the butter. When the pot gets warm, add the roast, and sear on all sides, about 8 minutes.

3 Distribute the carrots, celery, onion, jalapeño, and potatoes evenly around the roast. Add the stock, the Worcestershire sauce, and the garlic powder. Cover and cook for 20 minutes.

4 Switch to Warm and continue to cook covered for about 90 minutes until the roast reaches an internal temperature of at least 180°F.

5 Remove the roast to a cutting board to allow to rest for 15 minutes. Using a slotted spoon, transfer the vegetables to a serving dish. Discard all except 2 cups of liquid from pot. Add the flour and the remaining teaspoon of pepper and whisk continuously for about 2 minutes or until a sauce forms and thickens.

6 Thinly slice the beef and serve with vegetables and gravy.

Vegetables

Don't push those vegetables to the back of the refrigerator! Reportedly, folks aren't eating their veggies because of busy lifestyles and the extra time it takes to prep the food. But our bodies starve for those minerals and vitamins received by eating a variety of produce. Set aside a prep day and get everything chopped at the beginning of the week. That'll make it easy to grab a handful and add it to a dish or fix a quick side to accompany a main meal. Those marvelous veggies can be steamed to perfection in the rice cooker in minutes, retaining nutrients and ensuring tenderness. From Snow Peas with Bell Peppers and Swiss Chard with Raisins to Steamed Asparagus with Mustard-Dill Sauce and Buttered Mushrooms with Onions and Herbs, these dishes will have you reaching for veggies for every meal.

Steamed Napa Cabbage with Ham

Napa cabbage is not from California's wine country. It's known as Chinese cabbage in most of the world and is the primary ingredient in most kimchi preparations. A sweet cabbage, it pairs so nicely with the savory heartiness of ham.

Serves 4

- 4½ cups warm water, divided
- 1 teaspoon oyster sauce
- 1 (12–16-ounce) napa cabbage, separated into whole leaves and blanched
- 2 slices Canadian bacon, cut into thin strips

1 Add 4 cups of the water to the pot, cover, and set to Cook.

2 In a separate bowl, add the oyster sauce and the remaining ½ cup water and mix. Set aside.

3 Arrange the cabbage leaves on a plate and insert into the steamer basket with the Canadian bacon strips layered over and between the leaves. Pour the sauce over the cabbage.

4 When the water boils, put the steamer basket in the rice cooker and steam covered for 12 minutes or more until the cabbage leaves soften.

Snow Peas with Bell Peppers

Snow peas are a great vegetable for picky eaters. (Mainly kids, but you'll find a dearth of green on the dinner plates of many an adult as well.) The blend with the bell peppers is unusual and makes for a great bite.

Serves 2

1 tablespoon vegetable oil

1 clove garlic, peeled and finely minced

4 fresh shiitake mushroom caps, quartered

8 ounces snow peas

3 tablespoons water

½ medium green bell pepper, seeded and sliced

½ medium red bell pepper, seeded and sliced

¼ teaspoon ground white pepper

¼ teaspoon salt

1 Add the oil to the rice cooker, cover, and set to Cook. When the base of the pot gets warm, cook the minced garlic about 3 minutes until fragrant.

2 Add the mushrooms and cook for 3 minutes, covered and stirring occasionally.

3 Add the snow peas and continue cooking for 3 minutes more while gradually stirring in the water. Cover the rice cooker occasionally while cooking.

4 Add the bell peppers, mix well, and cook for 3–5 minutes; cover rice cooker occasionally while cooking. Add salt and white pepper and serve.

Know Your Cooking Sequence

The cooking sequence is important, and it helps to know your ingredients well. Snow peas take a longer time to cook than bell peppers. If you add them together, the snow peas might be perfectly cooked, but the bell peppers will be overdone.

Brussels Sprouts in Oyster Sauce

The oyster sauce in this dish brings out a fantastic but sometimes hard-to-unlock quality of the Brussels sprout: its surprising richness. The most important element of the prep for this recipe is to be sure your Brussels sprouts are completely cooked. Give them an extra minute or two, as too much time is much better than not enough with this vegetable.

Serves 2

- 8 Brussels sprouts, cut into halves
- 1 teaspoon oyster sauce
- 4½ cups warm water, divided
- 1 tablespoon vegetable oil
- 1 clove garlic, peeled and finely minced
- ½ teaspoon grated ginger
- ¼ teaspoon ground white pepper
- ¼ teaspoon ground black pepper

1. Place the Brussels sprouts on a plate that will fit into the steamer insert or basket. Set aside.

2. Add 4 cups of the water to the pot, cover, and set to Cook.

3. In a small bowl, combine the oyster sauce and ½ cup warm water and stir to mix. Set aside as sauce.

4. When the water in the rice cooker boils, insert the steamer basket and cook covered for 4 minutes until sprouts slightly soften. Drain excess water from the Brussels sprouts and set aside.

5. Clean out the rice cooker and wipe dry. Add the oil, cover, and set to Cook. When the base of the pot gets warm, add the garlic and ginger, followed by the Brussels sprouts placed cut-side down. Cook for 4 minutes, covering the rice cooker occasionally while cooking.

6. Add the sauce mixture, salt, and white and black pepper and mix well. Allow to simmer for 2 minutes, switching to Warm if the mixture bubbles too vigorously.

Prep Your Sprouts

Brussels sprouts rarely come in uniform sizes. To prepare the bigger sprouts for cooking, use a paring knife to cut a small cross at the bottom about ½-inch deep into the sprouts. This will ensure that the bigger sprouts cook faster than they otherwise would and all the sprouts will be cooked evenly.

Buttered Brussels Sprouts

As this recipe uses only a few basic ingredients, you can up the spice factor by mixing white and black pepper for added depth, flavor, and aroma. It's also worth the time and effort to make sure all the sprouts are cooked facedown.

Serves 2

8 Brussels sprouts, cut into halves

4 cups water

½ tablespoon butter

¼ teaspoon salt

¼ teaspoon ground black pepper

¼ teaspoon ground white pepper

1 Place the Brussels sprouts on a plate and set in the steamer basket. Set aside.

2 Add the water to the pot, cover the rice cooker, and set to Cook. When the water boils, insert the steamer basket and cook covered for 4 minutes until sprouts soften. Drain excess water from the Brussels sprouts and set aside.

3 Clean out the pot and wipe it dry. Add the butter, cover, and set to Cook. When the base of the pot gets warm, add the Brussels sprouts cut-side down and cook for about 3 minutes until tender. Before serving, add salt, black pepper, and white pepper. Toss well.

Kale with Mushrooms

Kale belongs to the same family as cabbage and Brussels sprouts. Leafy green vegetables are not easily found during winter months, but kale leads the pack in being high in vitamins, minerals, and various antioxidants. Add pine nuts to give an added crunch and texture to this otherwise soft-textured dish.

Serves 2

2 tablespoons extra-virgin olive oil

4 tightly packed cups finely chopped kale

4 ounces cremini mushroom caps, thinly sliced

½ cup water or as needed

¼ teaspoon salt

¼ teaspoon ground black pepper

1 Add the oil to the rice cooker, cover, and set to Cook. When the base of the pot gets warm, add the kale and the mushrooms and cook for about 3 minutes until the vegetables become tender. Add water if mixture is too dry.

2 Add the salt and pepper and toss well for another minute before serving.

Haricots Verts and Carrots

French green beans are the longer, thinner variety found in most groceries. They're more delicate and, on the stovetop at least, a little less forgiving than other kinds of green beans. You won't have to worry about that with this rice cooker dish, which turns them out just tender-crisp.

Serves 2

1 tablespoon olive oil

1 clove garlic, peeled and grated

1 teaspoon grated ginger

8 ounces French green beans, cut into finger-length pieces

1 cup peeled and shredded carrots

2 tablespoons water

½ teaspoon dried oregano

1 Add the oil to the pot, cover, and set to Cook. When the base of the pot gets warm, add the garlic and ginger, followed by the green beans and carrots. Cook for about 3 minutes, covering rice cooker occasionally while cooking.

2 Gradually stir in the water, cover rice cooker, and allow to simmer about 3 minutes until beans and carrots become tender and cook through, switching to Warm if the mixture bubbles too vigorously or dries out too quickly.

3 Before serving, sprinkle dried oregano over the vegetables.

Creamed Spinach

Many cooks like to blanch fresh spinach. This recipe calls for frozen spinach to avoid a common mistake in creamy spinach dishes, which happens when the blanching water isn't completely drained. Remember to do so if you go the fresh route.

Serves 2

1 tablespoon butter
¼ cup finely chopped shallots
½ pound frozen spinach, thawed
¼ cup heavy cream
¼ teaspoon salt
¼ teaspoon ground black pepper

1 Add the butter to the rice cooker, cover, and set to Cook. When the base of the pot gets warm, add the shallots and cook for about 3 minutes until shallots turn soft and slightly caramelize.

2 Add the spinach and cook stirring occasionally for about 5 minutes just until the liquid is released.

3 Slowly add the cream, cover, and cook 10 minutes or until cream reduces by almost half.

4 Switch to Warm and simmer for about 3 minutes, stirring occasionally until the mixture is thick and creamy.

5 Add the salt and pepper and stir well into the creamed mixture. Remove from the heat and serve immediately.

Swiss Chard with Raisins

Mature chard leaves and stalks are typically cooked to reduce the bitter flavor, especially in the stems. If the taste seems a little bitter, as chard dishes sometimes do, try adding a big splash of lemon juice.

Serves 2

2 tablespoons extra-virgin olive oil

½ cup thinly sliced onions

½ pound Swiss chard, leaves and stems separated, both coarsely chopped

¼ cup golden raisins, divided

½ cup water, divided

1 Add the oil to the rice cooker, cover, and set to Cook. When the base of the pot gets warm, add the onions and cook about 5 minutes until soft, covering intermittently.

2 Add the chard stems and cook for about 2 minutes. Add half the raisins and ¼ cup of the water and allow to simmer for 4 minutes covered until the stems soften.

3 Add the chard leaves and the remaining water and simmer covered until leaves become tender, about 4 minutes.

4 Sprinkle the remaining raisins over the vegetables before serving.

Okra Stew

This recipe is an adaptation of gumbo, the classic dish that is synonymous with Louisiana cuisine. Both are rooted in okra, onions, and bell peppers, and if you've always admired the dish but never given it a try, this rice cooker recipe is a great place to start.

Serves 2

- 2 tablespoons extra-virgin olive oil
- 2 cloves garlic, peeled and finely minced
- 1 medium onion, peeled and finely chopped
- 1 cup finely chopped green bell peppers
- 1 cup finely chopped red bell peppers
- ½ pound okra, sliced into ½-inch cubes
- 6 ounces white mushrooms, sliced
- ½ (14½-ounce) can diced tomatoes, with juice
- 2 bay leaves
- ¼ cup water
- ¼ teaspoon salt
- ¼ teaspoon ground black pepper
- ½ tablespoon all-purpose flour

1 Add the oil to the rice cooker, cover, and set to Cook. When the base of the pot gets warm, add the garlic, onion, and bell peppers. Cook about 5 minutes until tender, covering intermittently.

2 Add the okra, mushrooms, tomatoes, bay leaves, water, salt, and black pepper. Cover and allow to reach a slight simmer, stirring occasionally.

3 Switch rice cooker to Warm and simmer for about 30 minutes until mixture reaches a thick, stewy consistency.

4 Add the flour, stirring occasionally to further thicken the stew. Remove the bay leaves before serving.

Buttered Mushrooms with Onions and Herbs

Cremini mushrooms are richer in flavor and nutrients than white button mushrooms. They're also the same thing as "crimini" mushrooms—the name has its origins in a marketing campaign.

Serves 2

- 1 tablespoon extra-virgin olive oil
- 3 medium shallots, peeled and thinly sliced
- ½ pound cremini mushrooms, sliced
- ½ tablespoon butter
- ¼ teaspoon salt
- ¼ teaspoon ground black pepper
- ½ teaspoon dried oregano
- ½ teaspoon dried basil

1 Add the oil to the rice cooker, cover, and set to Cook. When the base of the pot gets warm, add the shallots and cook about 3 minutes until slightly soft.

2 Add the mushrooms and butter and cook for about 10 minutes, covering intermittently, until mushrooms turn soft. If the mix dries out too quickly, switch to Warm and continue to cook the mushrooms.

3 When mushrooms turn completely soft, add the salt, pepper, oregano, and basil. Mix well, cover rice cooker, set to Warm, and simmer for 2 minutes before serving hot.

Chickpeas with Peppers

For best results, dice the bell pepper instead of slicing so that the consistency of the final dish remains toothy and fresh.

Serves 2

- 2 tablespoons extra-virgin olive oil
- 3 medium shallots, peeled and thinly sliced
- 1 clove garlic, peeled and finely minced
- 1 teaspoon grated ginger
- 1 medium red bell pepper, seeded and diced
- 1 (14½-ounce) can chickpeas, drained, gently rinsed with water, then drained again
- ¼ teaspoon salt
- ¼ teaspoon ground black pepper
- 1 teaspoon finely chopped fresh cilantro, for garnish

1 Add the oil, cover, and set to Cook. When the base of the pot gets warm, add the shallots and cook about 3 minutes until soft. Add the garlic and ginger and cook about 3 minutes more until fragrant.

2 Add the bell peppers and chickpeas and cook for 6 minutes or until peppers turn tender, covering rice cooker while cooking. Season with the salt and black pepper to taste. Garnish with the cilantro.

Black Bean Patties

In addition to being perfect finger-friendly vegetarian snacks, these patties make healthy vegetarian burgers as well. Black beans are one of the best sources of protein available to anyone—vegan, vegetarian, or carnivore.

Serves 2

- 1 (15-ounce) can black beans, drained
- ½ medium green bell pepper, seeded and chopped
- ½ medium onion, cut into wedges, about ½-inch thick
- 3 cloves garlic, peeled
- 1 teaspoon ground cumin
- 1 teaspoon chili powder
- 1 egg
- 4 tablespoons vegetable oil, divided

1 Mash the beans in a large bowl with a fork until thick and pasty.

2 Add the bell peppers, onion, and garlic to a food processor or blender and process until finely grated.

3 Add the bell pepper mixture to the mashed beans and stir to combine, then add the cumin, chili powder, and egg. Use your fingers to evenly combine the mixture until it is sticky and holds together. Form into 4 patties and set aside.

4 Add 2 tablespoons oil to the rice cooker, cover, and set to Cook. When the base of the pot gets warm, add half the patties and cook each side for about 3 minutes or until browned. Cover rice cooker while cooking. Repeat with the remaining oil and patties.

Steamed Asparagus with Mustard-Dill Sauce

This side is so simple and easy to prepare it can almost make you mad that you didn't know about rice-cooker cooking sooner. This is a perfect side dish to go with salmon.

Serves 4

¼ cup mayonnaise

2 tablespoons Dijon mustard

2 teaspoons chopped fresh dill

1 tablespoon lemon juice

½ teaspoon lemon zest

¼ teaspoon plus ½ teaspoon salt, divided

1 cup water

1 bunch asparagus, trimmed of woody ends

2 tablespoons butter, cut into small dice

1 In a small bowl, whisk together the mayonnaise, mustard, dill, lemon juice, lemon zest, and ¼ teaspoon salt. Refrigerate covered while preparing the asparagus.

2 Add the water to the rice cooker. Put the asparagus into a steamer basket and place in the pot. Top with diced butter and sprinkle with remaining ½ teaspoon salt.

3 Cover rice cooker and set to Cook. Once the base of the cooker heats up, cook for 5 minutes. Uncover. The thickness of asparagus varies, so if it is still not cooked to your liking, cover, continue to cook, and check every 2 minutes.

4 Transfer the asparagus to a serving dish and drizzle with sauce. If the sauce has thickened in the refrigerator, just add a few drops of water to loosen until desired consistency is achieved.

Desserts and Drinks

We've saved the best and sweetest chapter for last. Think you can't cook cheesecake in a rice cooker? Oh yes you can. That 7-inch springform pan is the perfect size to make cheesecakes that will satisfy your sweet tooth. Often we just want a little dessert for a cheat meal or a little sweet bite after a family dinner, and the portions turned out by your rice cooker are ideal for just these situations. From Pumpkin Cheesecake with Gingersnap Crust and Blackberry Cobbler to Peaches and Coconut Cream Rice Pudding and Blueberry Bread Pudding, the desserts in this chapter are mouthwatering and will keep you coming back for more. And if you like your desserts in liquid form, don't skip the White Hot Chocolate, Chai Tea, or Spiced Mocha with Whipped Cream!

Pumpkin Cheesecake with Gingersnap Crust

If you've never had rice cooker cheesecake before—and really, who has?—you're in for a treat. This savory-sweet treat turns pumpkin pie inside out and upside down for an all-year dessert sure to make your guests swoon. Remember to start this the night before you serve it.

Serves 6

- 2 tablespoons vegetable oil
- 1 cup finely crushed gingersnaps
- 3 tablespoons butter, melted
- 8 ounces cream cheese, cubed and room temperature
- 2 tablespoons sour cream, room temperature
- 1 cup pumpkin purée
- ½ cup sugar
- ¼ teaspoon ground cinnamon
- ⅛ teaspoon ground nutmeg
- ½ teaspoon vanilla extract
- ⅛ teaspoon salt
- 2 large eggs, room temperature
- 2 cups water

1 Grease a 7-inch springform pan with vegetable oil and set aside.

2 In a small bowl, add gingersnaps and butter and stir until combined. Transfer the crumb mixture to the springform pan and press down along the bottom and about ⅓ of the way up the sides of the pan. Place a square of aluminum foil along the outside of the bottom of the pan and crimp up around the edges. Set aside.

3 Add the cream cheese, sour cream, pumpkin, sugar, cinnamon, nutmeg, vanilla, and salt to a large bowl or stand-mixer bowl and blend on medium speed until smooth. Slowly stir in the eggs and mix well. Pour into springform pan.

4 Pour water into rice cooker. Carefully place springform pan in the middle of cooker.

5 Cover and set to Cook. Once water reaches a boil, cook for 15 minutes. Switch heat to Warm and cook for 30 minutes more. Cool on the counter for 30 minutes.

6 Cover and refrigerate overnight to allow to set. Serve cold.

Caramelized All-Spiced Sweet Potato

For a variation, try using five-spice powder instead of cinnamon and ground nutmeg. Five-spice powder is a blend of star anise, cinnamon, cloves, fennel, and Szechuan pepper.

Serves 6

4 tablespoons vegetable oil

2 medium sweet potatoes, peeled and sliced about ¼ inch thick

¼ cup brown sugar

½ teaspoon ground cinnamon

½ teaspoon ground nutmeg

1 Add oil to the rice cooker, cover, and set to Cook. When the base of the pot gets warm, add the sweet potatoes. Cook for 8 minutes, covering intermittently until the sweet potatoes turn crisp on the outside but remain soft in the inside.

2 Add the brown sugar, switch rice cooker to Warm, and stir slowly and steadily until the sugar melts. When sugar completely caramelizes, in about 10 minutes, sprinkle in the cinnamon and nutmeg.

3 Cook for 8 minutes more, dish out, and serve warm.

Five-Spice or Seven-Spice Powder

While five-spice powder is mostly related to Chinese cooking, seven-spice powder is related to Japanese and sometimes Thai cuisines. In Japanese cuisine, seven-spice powder is a mixture that may include spices such as sesame seeds, dried orange or tangerine peel, poppy seeds, chili, and nori seaweed. In Thailand, seven-spice powder is a mixture that may be a blend of chili powder, garlic, ginger, coriander, star anise, cloves, and lemon peel.

Steamed Egg Cupcake

The oil called for in this recipe is used to lightly grease the ramekins so that the cupcakes don't stick and makes it easier to remove them after steaming. This cupcake recipe uses only a tablespoon of sugar, which you'll soon agree is hard to believe.

Yields 6 cupcakes

4 cups cold water

1 egg

1 tablespoon superfine (castor) sugar

¼ cup whole milk

2 ounces self-rising flour, sifted

1 tablespoon vegetable oil

1 Add the water to the cooker, cover, and set to Cook.

2 In a medium bowl, lightly whisk the egg and sugar. Slowly add the milk and stir to combine. Add the sifted flour and mix well, forming a pourable batter.

3 Use the vegetable oil to grease a round 6-cup muffin mold. Pour the mixture into cup molds, filling about 90 percent full. Cover the cups with foil and set aside on a plate that will fit in the steamer insert or basket.

4 When the water in the rice cooker boils, place steamer basket into the rice cooker, cover, and steam for about 15 minutes.

Pink Grapefruit Lemonade with Basil

The name alone is enough to make your mouth start to water, and wait until you try the basil-lemon combination. To bring in even more flavor, try it with a stalk of mashed or bruised lemongrass and serve it over a ½ cup of ice.

Serves 4

4 cups water
1 tablespoon sugar
2 tablespoons honey
½–1 cup freshly squeezed lemon juice, adjusted accordingly to sourness preference
1 cup fresh red grapefruit juice
½ cup roughly chopped fresh basil

1 Add the water to rice cooker, cover, and set to Cook. When water boils, add the sugar and honey and stir 5–8 minutes to dissolve. Switch off rice cooker and allow mixture to cool.

2 Add lemon and grapefruit juices into the sugar syrup and mix well. Pour into a jug for ease of serving the drink later.

3 Add the basil before serving.

Blackberry Cobbler

The cobbler was probably the first British colonial delicacy to become a staple back home. That's right; this dish was invented by American colonists. Delicious served warm with a scoop of vanilla ice cream or a dollop of whipped cream, this is the perfect dessert after a day of berry picking with the family.

Serves 6

2 cups fresh blackberries
1 teaspoon lemon juice
½ cup sugar
¾ cup all-purpose flour
1 teaspoon baking powder
⅛ teaspoon salt
4 tablespoons butter, melted
½ cup whole milk
2 cups water

1 Lightly grease a 7-cup glass bowl. Set aside.

2 In a medium bowl, add the blackberries, lemon juice, and sugar. Toss to combine and then refrigerate.

3 In a medium bowl, add the flour, baking powder, and salt and stir to combine. Stir in the butter and milk until combined. Spread the mixture into the bottom of the greased glass bowl. Pour the blackberries over the dough.

4 Pour the water into the rice cooker, insert the bowl, cover the pot, and set to Cook. When the water starts to boil, cook for 15 minutes. Switch heat to Warm and cook for 30 minutes more.

5 Remove the cobbler from the rice cooker and let sit for 15 minutes. Spoon into bowls and serve warm.

Orange Cheesecake with Chocolate Crust

The size of this dessert is perfect when that sweet tooth is screaming at you but you don't want to overdo it. There will be no leftovers here, and with one-pot cooking, your cleanup is a cinch.

Serves 6

1 cup finely crushed chocolate graham crackers

3 tablespoons butter, melted

12 ounces cream cheese, cubed and room temperature

2 tablespoons sour cream, room temperature

½ cup sugar

2 large eggs, room temperature

2 teaspoons orange zest

1 tablespoon freshly squeezed orange juice

1 teaspoon vanilla extract

⅛ teaspoon salt

2 cups water

1 Grease a 7-inch springform pan and set aside.

2 In a small bowl, add the graham crackers and butter and stir until combined. Transfer the crumb mixture to the springform pan and press down along the bottom and about ⅓ of the way up the sides of the pan. Place a square of aluminum foil along the outside of the bottom of the pan and crimp up around the edges. Set aside.

3 In a medium bowl, add the cream cheese, sour cream, and sugar and stir until smooth. Slowly add the eggs and mix until combined. Add the zest, orange juice, vanilla, and salt and stir until combined. Pour into the spring-form pan.

4 Pour the water into rice cooker. Carefully place the springform pan in the middle of cooker.

5 Cover and set to Cook. When the water starts to boil, cook for 15 minutes. Switch heat to Warm and cook for 30 minutes. Cool on the counter for 30 minutes, then cover and refrigerate overnight to allow to set. Serve cold.

Peaches and Coconut Cream Rice Pudding

The traditional Southern peaches and cream combination receives a tropical twist in this recipe by adding coconut milk. This silky and sweet dish shows off your rice cooker at its surprisingly adaptable, efficient best.

Serves 4

1 (13½-ounce) can coconut milk

3 cups peeled and diced peaches

½ cup jasmine rice

⅓ cup sugar

¼ teaspoon ground cinnamon

1 teaspoon vanilla extract

⅛ teaspoon ground nutmeg

⅛ teaspoon salt

¾ cup water

½ cup whole milk

1 Add all ingredients except the whole milk to the rice cooker. Cover and switch to Cook.

2 Let cook until the cooker switches itself to Warm. Add the whole milk. Stir and serve.

Chai Tea

Impress your guests with coffeehouse-quality fresh chai tea. The spices will warm your tummy and fill your kitchen with a beautiful aroma. Once you're handy with this one, you may find yourself brewing all sorts of whole-leaf teas based on this recipe.

Serves 4

3 cups water
4 black tea bags
3 cardamom pods
4 whole cloves
1 (3-inch) cinnamon stick
4 whole allspice berries
¼ teaspoon ground nutmeg
1 cup whole milk
¼ cup sugar

1 Add the water, tea bags, cardamom, cloves, cinnamon, allspice, and nutmeg to rice cooker. Bring to a boil.

2 Reduce heat to Warm. Simmer for 5 minutes.

3 Add the milk and sugar and let steep for an additional 5 minutes. Strain and discard solids. Press any additional liquid and flavor out of the tea bags. Serve warm, chilled, or on ice.

Mexican Hot Cocoa

The chili powder and cayenne may seem weird if you've never tried them like this, but once you do, you'll never go back. These flavors play so nicely with chocolate and just deepen the yummy experience with this warm cup of comfort.

Serves 4

5 cups whole milk
¼ cup unsweetened cocoa
½ cup semisweet chocolate chips
¼ teaspoon chili powder
⅛ teaspoon cayenne pepper
⅛ teaspoon ground nutmeg
⅛ teaspoon sea salt
1 (3-inch) cinnamon stick
2 teaspoons vanilla extract
¼ cup sugar
1 cup whipped cream

1 Place all ingredients except the whipped cream into rice cooker and set to Cook. Heat until mixture just starts to boil.

2 Switch the cooker to Warm and simmer for 10 minutes. Discard the cinnamon stick.

3 Ladle into 4 coffee mugs and top with the whipped cream.

Brown Sugar and Cinnamon Bread Pudding

Try this tasty dessert heated up with a scoop of vanilla ice cream or a few dollops of whipped cream. Bread pudding is also tasty cold in the morning with a nice cup of tea or coffee. Any way you serve it up, this recipe wins a lot of morning smiles.

Serves 6

- 4 cups cubed cinnamon brown sugar bread, dried out overnight
- 1½ cups half-and-half
- 2 large eggs
- ½ teaspoon vanilla extract
- ⅓ cup brown sugar
- ½ teaspoon ground cinnamon
- ⅛ teaspoon salt
- ⅛ teaspoon ground nutmeg
- 2 teaspoons lemon zest
- ¼ cup raisins
- 3 tablespoons butter, cut into 6 pats
- 2 cups water

1. Lightly grease a 7-cup glass dish. Set aside.

2. Place the bread in a medium bowl. Set aside.

3. In a small bowl, whisk together the half-and-half, eggs, vanilla, brown sugar, cinnamon, salt, nutmeg, lemon zest, and raisins. Pour over the bread and toss. Transfer to the greased glass dish. Push the pats of butter into the top of the mixture.

4. Pour the water into the rice cooker. Insert the bread pudding dish, cover, and set to Cook. When the base of the cooker is warm, cook for 16 minutes. Reduce heat to Warm and continue to heat for 25 minutes. Remove the dish from the rice cooker and serve or refrigerate overnight to allow bread pudding to set.

Blueberry Bread Pudding

With so many breads available to us these days, there are lots of bread pudding options available. Experiment with the flavors for a variety of desserts. Also, if you can't get your hands on specialty bread, go ahead and use white bread, challah, or the all-time favorite, brioche.

Serves 6

- 4 cups cubed blueberry swirl bread, dried overnight
- 1½ cups half-and-half
- 2 large eggs
- ½ teaspoon vanilla extract
- ⅓ cup sugar
- ⅛ teaspoon salt
- ⅛ teaspoon ground nutmeg
- 2 teaspoons orange zest
- ¼ cup blueberries, overflowing measurement, plus 2 tablespoons, divided
- 3 tablespoons butter, cut into 6 pats
- 2 cups water

1 Lightly grease a 7-cup glass dish. Set aside.

2 Place the bread in a medium bowl. Set aside.

3 In a small bowl, whisk together the half-and-half, eggs, vanilla, sugar, salt, nutmeg, and orange zest. Toss in the overflowing ¼ cup blueberries. Pour over the bread and toss. Transfer to the greased glass dish. Push the pats of butter into top of mixture.

4 Pour the water into rice cooker. Insert the bread pudding dish, cover, and set to Cook. When the base of the cooker is warm, cook for 16 minutes.

5 Reduce heat to Warm and cook for 25 minutes. Remove dish from rice cooker, top with remaining 2 tablespoons blueberries, and serve or refrigerate overnight to allow bread pudding to set.

Spiced Mocha with Whipped Cream

The richness of this spiced mocha will make cold-weather sipping your new favorite pastime. Try it with any of the bread puddings in this book, or with a slice of pumpkin cheesecake if you're ready to really let go.

Serves 4

- 3 cups water
- 2 tablespoons instant espresso powder
- 2 tablespoons unsweetened cocoa powder
- ⅛ teaspoon salt
- 4 whole allspice berries
- 1 star anise pod
- 4 cardamom pods
- 1 (3-inch) cinnamon stick
- 2 cups whole milk
- ¼ cup sugar
- 1 cup whipped cream

1 Add the water, espresso powder, cocoa powder, salt, allspice, star anise, cardamom, and cinnamon to rice cooker. Cover and set to Cook. Bring to a boil.

2 Switch the cooker to Warm and simmer for 10 minutes.

3 Add the milk and sugar and steep for an additional 3 minutes. Strain and discard solids. Ladle into 4 mugs and top with the whipped cream.

White Hot Chocolate

This white, hot delight can certainly be enjoyed year-round, but you can add a little holiday cheer by adding a peppermint stick to stir your marshmallows. It's a seasonal classic sure to tide any little ones over until dinner, and it leaves your stovetop free for all your other holiday dishes.

Serves 4

5 cups whole milk
1 cup white chocolate chips
⅛ teaspoon salt
2 tablespoons sugar
1 teaspoon vanilla extract
1 cup mini marshmallows

1 Place all ingredients except the marshmallows into rice cooker and set to Cook. Heat until mixture begins to boil.

2 Switch cooker to warm and simmer for 10 minutes. Stir to ensure the white chocolate chips are melted. Simmer for an additional 2 minutes if more melting is required.

3 Ladle into 4 coffee mugs and top with the mini marshmallows.

US/Metric Conversion Chart

VOLUME CONVERSIONS

US Volume Measure	Metric Equivalent
⅛ teaspoon	0.5 milliliter
¼ teaspoon	1 milliliter
½ teaspoon	2 milliliters
1 teaspoon	5 milliliters
½ tablespoon	7 milliliters
1 tablespoon (3 teaspoons)	15 milliliters
2 tablespoons (1 fluid ounce)	30 milliliters
¼ cup (4 tablespoons)	60 milliliters
⅓ cup	90 milliliters
½ cup (4 fluid ounces)	125 milliliters
⅔ cup	160 milliliters
¾ cup (6 fluid ounces)	180 milliliters
1 cup (16 tablespoons)	250 milliliters
1 pint (2 cups)	500 milliliters
1 quart (4 cups)	1 liter (about)

WEIGHT CONVERSIONS

US Weight Measure	Metric Equivalent
½ ounce	15 grams
1 ounce	30 grams
2 ounces	60 grams
3 ounces	85 grams
¼ pound (4 ounces)	115 grams
½ pound (8 ounces)	225 grams
¾ pound (12 ounces)	340 grams
1 pound (16 ounces)	454 grams

OVEN TEMPERATURE CONVERSIONS

Degrees Fahrenheit	Degrees Celsius
200 degrees F	95 degrees C
250 degrees F	120 degrees C
275 degrees F	135 degrees C
300 degrees F	150 degrees C
325 degrees F	160 degrees C
350 degrees F	180 degrees C
375 degrees F	190 degrees C
400 degrees F	205 degrees C
425 degrees F	220 degrees C
450 degrees F	230 degrees C

BAKING PAN SIZES

American	Metric
8 x 1½ inch round baking pan	20 x 4 cm cake tin
9 x 1½ inch round baking pan	23 x 3.5 cm cake tin
11 x 7 x 1½ inch baking pan	28 x 18 x 4 cm baking tin
13 x 9 x 2 inch baking pan	30 x 20 x 5 cm baking tin
2 quart rectangular baking dish	30 x 20 x 3 cm baking tin
15 x 10 x 2 inch baking pan	30 x 25 x 2 cm baking tin (Swiss roll tin)
9 inch pie plate	22 x 4 or 23 x 4 cm pie plate
7 or 8 inch springform pan	18 or 20 cm springform or loose bottom cake tin
9 x 5 x 3 inch loaf pan	23 x 13 x 7 cm or 2 lb narrow loaf or pâté tin
1½ quart casserole	1.5 liter casserole
2 quart casserole	2 liter casserole

Index